Warwickshire's Murderous Women

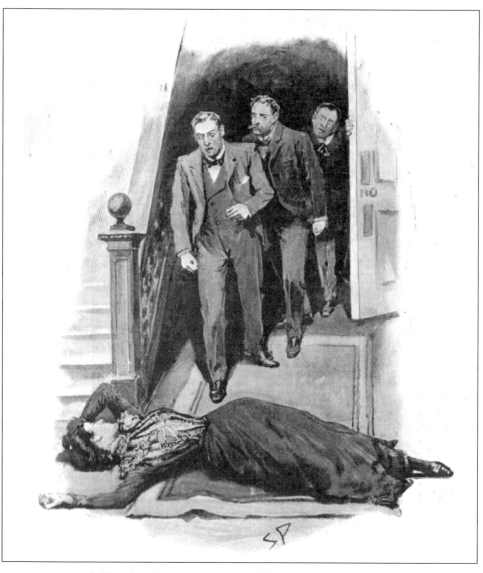

In Victorian times women were usually the victims, but not always.
Strand Magazine

WARWICKSHIRE'S MURDEROUS WOMEN

Nineteenth Century Killers

Nick Billingham

Wharncliffe Books

First published in Great Britain in 2008 by
Wharncliffe Books
an imprint of
Pen & Sword Books Ltd
47 Church Street
Barnsley
South Yorkshire
S70 2AS

© Nick Billingham 2008

ISBN: 978 184563 063 8

Typeset in Plantin and ITC Benguiat by
Mousemat Design Limited

Printed and bound in Great Britain by CPI UK

Pen & Sword Books Ltd incorporates the imprints of
Pen & Sword Aviation, Pen & Sword Maritime,
Pen & Sword Military, Wharncliffe Local History,
Pen and Sword Select, Pen and Sword Military Classics
and Leo Cooper.

For a complete list of Pen & Sword titles please contact
PEN & SWORD BOOKS LIMITED
47 Church Street, Barnsley, South Yorkshire,
S70 2AS, England
E-mail: enquiries@pen-and-sword.co.uk
Website: www.pen-and-sword.co.uk

Contents

Introduction

This is the fourth book about fouls deeds that I have written. It has been something of a sharp learning curve, starting from virtual ignorance of just how awful people can be to each other, to the discovery of my great great grandfather's murder over something as trivial as leaving a bottle of port uncorked; and then on into the dark underbelly of Victorian Birmingham. Onwards into the sunlit fields of South Warwickshire where, in my second book, I discovered that life in villages and small towns could be just as unpleasant as the back streets of any industrial city. By the time I finished the third book, back to those dark city streets, I noticed a distinct trend starting to emerge.

If nothing else, man's inhumanity to woman stands out vividly through the annals of crime. My second book of Birmingham crimes is virtually entirely composed of sad, bad or basically barking blokes killing their wives and girlfriends. Jealousy is the usual motive. John Grayson Farquhar spotted his beloved housekeeper, to whom he had already proposed, talking to some young man, so he shot her. John Thompson, who wasn't quite such a gentleman, cut his housekeeper's throat for exactly the same reason. The year 1861 was really bad for housekeepers. The book is simply stuffed with similar cases. The methods may vary: knives, guns and the perennial favourite – a cut-throat razor (named as much for its track record as appearance), but it's the women who are on the receiving end of such sudden and mindless violence.

It struck me that it must be time to redress the balance. Surely this violence was not all one sided. Didn't the ladies occasionally get the first blow in, slip something a tad toxic into dear hubby's tea? In short, make them really wish that they had done the washing up just once in a while. I took heart from the case of Maria Woolley who, after years of violent abuse, picked up the poker and flung it at her no good husband when he got back from the pub. It flew straight into his eye and killed him. It must be said that she hadn't intended to kill him and was utterly horrified at the result, but it did suggest that women weren't always going to give up without a fight. This was the genesis of this book and the start of an exploration of the women who became killers in the Victorian period.

As with any exploration, the first things to leave behind are the pre-conceptions we already have firmly fixed. The real world of crime is far removed from famous television detectives solving fiendishly complicated plots by master criminals of unparalleled intelligence. Murder is an irrational thing, born out of madness; your truly intelligent criminal has no need to kill someone when a cunningly crafted contract will achieve almost exactly the same result without making a mess on the carpet. Manslaughter is virtually always a sudden blaze of fury and

---

THROWING A WIFE DOWN A WELL AT ERDINGTON.— *William Dabbs*, 52, bricklayer, was indicted for having wilfully attempted to murder his wife, Eliza Dabbs, at Erdington, on the 30th of November.—Mr. Ewens-Bennett prosecuted; prisoner was undefended.—The evidence went to show that the prosecutrix and prisoner, who lived at Short Heath, near Erdington, had been quarrelling during the whole of the evening of the 30th November. Earlier in the day they had been to Birmingham. About eleven o'clock at night Mrs. Dabbs went to the back door, and her husband, who followed, seized her by the shoulders, and "twirled" her round and threw her into the well, which was about five yards distant. The well was eight feet deep, and contained three feet of water. The woman screamed for help, and her niece, who had been ordered to go to bed earlier in the evening, ran downstairs and begged prisoner, who was sitting in the kitchen, to render help. He, however, refused, saying, "Let the b—— die." The niece then ran to obtain the help of

---

A fairly typical example of crime in the city.

Warwickshire Advertiser and Leamington Spa Gazette

when the red mist fades, the killer is found sitting in a bemused daze wondering what all the fuss is about and whether the '1001 Handy Household Hints' says anything about getting blood off ceilings.

The pre-conceptions about female killers seem to revolve around poison for some reason. Lucrezia Borgia seems to be the role model for this: a nice dish of mushroom soup and the path is cleared for your dynastic ambitions. Fortunately, life in Warwickshire has been singularly free of such power politics and the few poisonings that have been recorded have been committed by men as well as women. William Beamish of Coventry went to the gallows in 1861 for putting arsenic in his family's dinner and then having a party with his girlfriend (the housekeeper – I told you 1861 was a bad year) whilst his little daughter was being buried – the cad. Of course, said housekeeper may well have been in on the plot to kill off his wife so she could marry William, but the jury cleared her of any involvement in the poisoning bit. As we will see, poisoning can be difficult to prove, or even diagnose, especially in an era with very primitive forensic science. Naturally the proficient poisoner never gets caught and probably relishes all the sympathy for her unlucky choice of various husbands who promptly pop their clogs. History seems to show that such pre-meditated acts are extremely rare. One preconception widespread in the nineteenth century was that arsenic couldn't be traced. It was tasteless and very easy to obtain, but it *could* be traced, even in tiny amounts. There are several cases where a case of natural causes turns out to be a murder on closer examination - much to the surprised annoyance of the wife.

There are several types of killings that seem to be associated with women. The first of these is infanticide. It certainly isn't a pleasant topic, but it is one that appears all too frequently in the pages of old newspapers. Men did kill their children, but mostly they were at work and it was the women who were left at home to cope with a screaming infant with little food and no money until something inside went snap. In Victorian times infant mortality was far greater than it is today. Young children died of dozens of diseases that today we don't even worry about. Diphtheria, whooping cough, measles and smallpox all slaughtered thousands of children; and for anyone wondering whether modern vaccines are a good idea just read the pages of the newspapers from an era before they were invented. Children were almost expected to die, and there was very rarely a detailed inquest into yet another dead child. There is little doubt that hundreds of babies were shaken to death but the crime was never identified. However, there were cases that did hit the headlines and often reveal callous and heartless parents to whom children were a mere nuisance.

Abortion is another uniquely female activity of the Victorian era. I have absolutely no intention of going into the arguments surrounding the morality of such a practise. There are so many shades of grey and individual circumstances that the subject is a moral minefield. The Victorians considered it a serious crime, insisted that it was illegal and so opened the door for the shady world of the back street abortionist. These were usually women, often midwives and frequently so utterly incompetent that the woman having the abortion died as well as the foetus. There isn't any moral ambiguity about these cases, and so I consider them relevant for this book.

Further on from abortion is the matter of concealment of birth. As I have been writing this book there has been a case in all the headlines of the local papers. Baby Lily was found in the River Alne and a massive search began to find the mother. In the nineteenth century cases of this nature were far more common and the coroner had to make the same decision: was the child killed or was it a stillbirth? Forensic science was far more primitive in those days and social attitudes somewhat different. The cases show the desperate conditions that young women faced, utterly degrading poverty and often a complete ignorance about what was happening to them.

In many of these distressing events the courts were surprisingly merciful and understanding. Victorian justice could be incredibly harsh, with ferocious penalties for quite trivial offences, and yet many of these sad stories are treated with a sympathy that comes as a real surprise. The tale of Mary Dolan in Birmingham is a good example of how Victorian courts sometimes went out of their way to be lenient to abused women. She was a button maker and married to Patrick Dolan. He was an abusive man who thought nothing of beating her to within an inch of her life. By 10 April 1863 she had had enough and intended to leave him. According to their son Michael they spent the whole day arguing, and this culminated in him throwing some chairs at her. She retaliated by hurling a large seashell at him. It bounced off his skull leaving three deep wounds. Within a couple of days he was taken to hospital with septicaemia from these cuts. In a world without antibiotics this was fatal and he died on 16 April. Mary Dolan was charged with murder. She pleaded that she had acted in self defence but the jury still found her guilty. They did recommend mercy to the judge who, rather than send her to the gallows, sentenced her to two months in prison.

For the most part the killings that have found their way into this book defy classification. They are random insights that open a brief but detailed window into the nineteenth century, moments of history that have been preserved in the records because of their singular character. It turns out that some women are just as sad, bad or bonkers as men, but far fewer of them resorted to violence and often the provocation that they endured for years before the event should have made them a saint not a sinner.

Just once in a while Victorian Women fought back.
Strand Magazine

CHAPTER 1

Ann Heytrey
ASHOW
1819

She must kill her mistress.

There are some cases that seem to defy all logic and reason, a sudden outburst of extreme violence striking like lightning from a clear sky. The case of Ann Heytrey is one of these. There was no warning, no telltale signs of simmering hatred or tension, just a strange, inexplicable compulsion to kill.

Ann Heytrey got a job working as a kitchen maid at the Dial House in the parish of Ashow on Lady Day 1818. The household consisted of Joseph and Sarah Dormer, six children and another three servants. The Dial House, named because of the sundial on its wall, was quite some distance from the village centre. It was near the crossroads on the Warwick to Kenilworth route, not far from Chesford Grange. Right on the edge of the parish, it was one of the more isolated farms.

Ann was only twenty. She had been raised in the village of Charlecote, between Stratford and Wellesbourne. Her father was an agricultural labourer but when he died his wife was left to bring up her two children, Ann and her brother Thomas, in

A Victorian map showing the location of Ashow.

The author

desperate poverty, relying on the local parish to keep body and soul together. Life in rural England during the Napoleonic Wars was difficult, to say the least. There was widespread poverty and even though many men had gone to fight the French; farm wages remained low. New fangled agricultural practices reduced the number of workers needed on many farms. When the wars ended in 1815, the returning soldiers flooded the labour market and drove down wages still further. The gentlemen farmers of the time were building massive farm holdings and enclosing the common lands so that the ordinary labourers could no longer collect firewood or wild fruits. For a widow and her children life was unrelentingly grim. It was a time when a loaf of bread cost a day's wages and the temptation to slip into a life of crime was as strong as the penalties were severe.

Early in 1819, Ann Heytrey attempted to steal some notes from the Dial House. These were almost certainly bank notes. Her brother Thomas had already gained a reputation as a crook and could probably have passed them off amongst his underworld contacts. As it was Ann was caught before the notes could be spirited away, Mr Dormer charged her with the attempted theft. This was a capital offence, so Ann would have been dragged on a hurdle through the streets of Warwick before being hung. Public execution was the sentence for many offences; the alternative was transportation to the newly expanding colonies. For the most part, unless the offence was that of murder, death sentences were almost always commuted to transportation.

Ann was extremely fortunate that Sarah Dormer spoke up for her at her trial and the charges were laid aside. In a very real sense Ann Heytrey owed her mistress her life. It was a debt that she seemed to take seriously, later remarking: 'I liked my mistress so much I would have got up at any hour of the night to serve her.'

Ann was now twenty-one and was slightly shorter than average but a stoutly built girl with striking dark brown hair and eyes. People said her face was 'comely' although not very beautiful. Her hands had been coarsened by the endless hours of toil in the kitchen and laundry of the Dial House. The household seemed to function in a perfectly normal manner. Mr

Joseph Dormer was engaged in business and managing his agricultural estate. Sarah Dormer managed the household. Every farm of this size was a little village in its own right. The Dormer's six children ranged from about five to seventeen. Ann tended the kitchen and laundry whilst Richard Smith, John Branstone and J Barnacle looked after the carts, wagons and grounds.

The Parish Wake on Sunday 29 August 1819 was a special day for the village, a festival of thanksgiving. Mr Joseph Dormer invited some of his business colleagues to attend the festivities. The two Mr Brays of Coventry came for the day and Mr Dormer took them to see the wake whilst Mrs Dormer stayed in the house arranging lunch. Mr Thomas Harris and Mr William Hinde had come to join the family as well.

After lunch the group spent the afternoon drinking tea and chatting until about six o'clock. It was a fine evening and the two gentlemen went for a walk to Mr Aldridge's house, Thickthorn, taking all the children with them. Sarah stayed in

Ashow village centre today, still a peaceful island of tranquility in mid Warwickshire. The author

the house with Ann Heytrey. All the other servants had gone to the wake and silence descended on the house.

Two village children knocked at the back door and Sarah invited them in and gave them each a glass of wine and some cucumbers to take home with them. The children left by the front door and set off for another house to see what the other gentry might give them. Sarah and Ann went out into the kitchen garden and spent ten minutes picking some more cucumbers for supper. They returned to the house and Sarah went into the best kitchen. She put on her spectacles and sat down beside the window to read a book.

Miss E Jaggard and her friends were walking back to her house, The Forge. She clearly saw Sarah sitting by the window. After a few moments she noticed Ann, wearing a deep red dress with a coarse apron, walk out into the road, look down it towards the village as though to see if any of the family were returning, and then walk back into the house.

Sarah Dormer was sitting reading her book with the late August sunshine streaming in through the window. Her wealthy husband and his guests were out in the village enjoying the wake, her children and the other guests taking a pleasant stroll and her maidservant was busy chopping up onions and cucumbers in the scullery. It was a moment of peace and tranquillity in her busy life.

Ann Heytrey, midway through chopping up the onions, was suddenly overcome by such a powerful urge that she simple had to obey it. She must kill her mistress. Ann deliberately put down the knife and slowly walked from the scullery to the kitchen. Sarah looked up at her unexpected presence. Ann smashed her fist full into her mouth, so hard that it knocked out two of her front teeth and flung her to the floor. Ann kicked and punched her as she lay helpless on the cold flagstones. Whimpering in pain and fear, shocked to the very core, Sarah struggled up and ran into the hall. Here she could have bolted out of the door and out into the road, to seek help from the various travellers like Miss Jaggard. In her panic Sarah Dormer turned to the stairs and sought sanctuary in the supposed privacy and safety of her bedroom.

Ann Heytrey returned to the scullery like an automaton, her trance-like mood had shut down all her emotions and left nothing of her character but a deliberate and deadly purpose. She had to kill. She picked up the sharp kitchen knife and returned to the hall. Ann followed the spots of blood across the hall and up the stairs. In the absolute silence of the empty house Sarah Dormer could hear the steady tread reaching the landing, cornering the cowering Sarah in her bedroom. After what must have seemed an interminable wait Ann Heytrey burst into the room and rushed at Sarah with the knife. Sarah attempted to fend off the furious blows, and had her hands lacerated down to the bone in the one-sided struggle. She dropped to her knees, overwhelmed by the relentless assault. Ann grabbed her hair, wrenched back her head and slashed at her throat, first cutting across her jaw and then repeatedly carving the blade through her windpipe until the steel reached her spine. Sarah's blood poured from the wound onto Ann's apron and red dress, she fell backwards to the floor, her life ebbing away with each weakening spurt. Ann then took a black cap and placed it under her shoulder, positioned the knife carefully beside her arm and, quietly closing the bedroom door, went downstairs. There was blood dripping from her apron.

Ann removed the blood-steeped apron and went out of the back door to the washhouse further down the yard. There she quite sensibly put it in to soak. Then she went back into the house and made a desultory effort to clean up the spots of blood in the hall and stairs with a towel. She took this out to the tub as well. Standing alone in the hall in the now utterly silent house, the strange compulsion that had come over Ann suddenly left her. The relentless fury subsided as quickly as it came, leaving her confused and shivering in terror. The whole tragedy took no more than a few minutes.

The children arrived back from their walk at ten past seven, just a little later. Elizabeth, the oldest, at sixteen, opened the back door and found Ann standing in the passageway. She was shaking and sweating heavily. She appeared distressed and went out of the door without saying a word. Elizabeth, Joseph, Mary and Harriett stood in the hall wondering what on earth was the matter with her. Ann came back in and Elizabeth asked her if anyone had come to the house. Ann told her that nobody had, but seemed very confused. Elizabeth then asked where her mother was and Ann told her that she had gone out, towards

Ashow. Joseph, the fifteen-year-old, suddenly noticed something strange in the gloom of the narrow hall. He pointed to the drops of blood on the floor. Elizabeth looked too and asked Ann:

'Nancy, what is this?'

'Oh, nothing,' came the reply.

Elizabeth told her to get a mop and clear it up. Her younger sister Harriett called out for her mother and then asked Ann where she was. This time she said that Sarah was out in the garden picking cucumbers. Elizabeth and Mary went upstairs to their rooms. Elizabeth noticed that the door to her mother's room on the left of the landing was closed. She went into her room opposite. Mary, being only fourteen, really wanted to see her mother and tell her all about what she had seen at the wake. She opened the bedroom door.

Her screams echoed throughout the house and even into the road outside.

'Murder, my mother is murdered!'

Out on the road a surgeon by the name of Mr Bodington heard the frantic shrieks and spurred his horse right across the garden to the front door. Downstairs, Joseph ran out to the woodshed and grabbed the nearest weapon he could find, a garden fork, and raced up the stairs. Ann Heytrey followed him. They stood staring at the ruined body of Sarah Dormer weltering in a pool of blood. It dawned on Joseph that Ann Heytrey's hands were covered in blood.

He grabbed Ann's hand and stared at it. Then he dragged her downstairs and out into the yard. He slapped her hard across the face.

'You have no occasion to pull me, I'll go where you have a mind to take me,' she muttered.

Joseph dragged her into the road and shouted:

'You have killed my mother.'

Ann just shrugged her shoulders.

In the house full of panicked children Mr Bodington took charge. He examined Sarah Dormer, but there was nothing his skills could do for her; she was dead. He decided it would be best to seal up the room and call the constable. Word was spreading rapidly around the district as the other people on the road spread the rumour. Samuel Turner had taken charge of

Ann from Joseph in an effort to stop Joseph from ramming the fork straight through her there and then. He held her until Thomas Bellerby, the constable from Kenilworth arrived at half past eight. He asked Ann if she was the servant who had killed her mistress.

'They say so, but I am not.' The constable was not convinced; her hands were still covered in blood. He asked her if the apron she had on was the one she was wearing earlier. No she said it was not, and the other apron was hanging on the woodshed door. Thomas Bellerby escorted the stunned Ann Heytrey to Warwick Gaol.

The next morning, Mr Bodington and another surgeon, Mr Hiron, returned to conduct a proper autopsy. Thomas Bellerby came back to examine the scene as well. He found the blood-

Ashow church, tucked away down a wooded footpath. The author

stained apron and towel soaking in the wash house. There appeared to be no logical motive for the murder other than robbery. Ann's brother, Thomas, already had a reputation for being a petty criminal even though he had a reasonably well paid job as a blacksmith on a farm near Stratford. Thomas was arrested that afternoon and questioned. He had no idea why Ann had suddenly murdered her mistress. It was all as much a mystery to him as everyone else.

It was shock of the arrest and interrogation of her brother that brought Ann out of her sullen silence. When Constable Bellerby told her that he had been taken into custody she replied:

'What a thing it is to bring my friends into trouble. Neither my brother nor no other man had to do with the murder.'

'If you say that, you know who did it,' said the constable.

Ann then described how she was suddenly and completely overwhelmed by the urge to kill her mistress. She then told him every detail of the assault in the kitchen and the brutal violence in the bedroom. Thomas Bellerby was aghast at her words; he just couldn't believe what he was hearing.

'Did she make resistance?'

'Very little.'

'Did she cry out?'

'No.'

'Why did you not run away?'

'I was so confused I did not know what to do.'

'Had your mistress done or said something in the course of the day to offend you?'

'She had never given me an angry word.'

At long last her impenetrable emotional paralysis snapped. Ann broke down in tears and sobbed that she liked her mistress so much that she would have done anything for her. She just could not explain the strange and sudden compulsion that had made her kill her.

At the Lent Assizes the following spring Ann Heytrey was found guilty of petty treason and sentenced to death. Over the months she still had not discovered a reason for her attack on Sarah Dormer. Racked with guilt and confusion, she wrote to Elizabeth Dormer on 10 April, just a few days before her execution was due:

Dear Miss Dolmar,
I take the liberty of addressing you with this epistle for the last
time and I am heartily sorry for the sorrowful misfortune as
has happened which I hope the Lord in his mercies will forgive
me and I was very sorry to see you look so bad. I did not know
you when you was called up. I hope you will forgive me for
what I have done as my life will pay for the unfortunate deed.
Oh may the Almighty be your comfort and may he pardon me
my sins. Miss Dolmar I ask your forgiveness and the family's
at large…

On Wednesday 12 April, Ann Heytrey was bound to a hurdle
outside Warwick Gaol and dragged to the scaffold. It wasn't a
great distance. In 1820 all the executions took place just outside
the gates of the gaol. A priest was in constant attendance,
begging her to explain why she had killed Sarah Dormer. No
one could conceive that there wasn't some rational motive for
this sudden murder. Right up to the last moment Ann insisted
that the killing was because of that strange compulsion and that
she had no other motive.

The scene of Ann Heytrey's execution outside Warwick Gaol. The author

Thousands of people had come from all over the county to see the execution. These were normally rather riotous affairs with the crowds jeering and mocking those condemned to death. On this occasion however the crowd fell silent as she was led up the steps to her doom. She begged forgiveness once again, and the trap fell. Within a few minutes she had been strangled. An hour later her body was cut down. As was the custom in those days, her body was to be given to medical science. It was handed over to none other than Mr Bodington of Kenilworth. Perhaps he hoped to find an explanation for the senseless killing during his dissection, but he never found one.

In a bizarre twist of fate, it was less than a year later that Ann's brother, Thomas, was executed on exactly the same scaffold. He was implicated in a violent highway robbery and duly sentenced to death.

The Dormer family graves. Joseph and Sarah's is in the centre foreground.

The author

CHAPTER 2

Esther Bates and Friends
BIRMINGHAM
1822

*He was paralysed from the waist down
and covered in massive bruising.*

John Archer of Alcester was a twenty-eight-year-old man who had to travel to Birmingham on business every now and then. History doesn't record what it was that took him up there, but it was quite possibly the manufacture of pins and needles. Several of the towns along the River Arrow used water mills to power grinding wheels. Redditch, Studley and Alcester all had small factories transforming steel wire into pins and these found a ready market in the big city.

On 26 May 1822, John made his way to Birmingham to sell his wares and by 5 in the afternoon was all done. He had over 17 shillings in his pocket as a result, 85p in modern money, but the equivalent of a month's wages in those days. He felt he deserved a drink and so he popped into a pub in Dale End for a quick one to celebrate. This was a mistake.

The pubs in Dale End had a certain reputation, and not a good one either. Usually described as dens of infamy and vice, they were home to the dregs of Birmingham's low life. Thieves, prostitutes and worse haunted their ill-lit bars looking for a sucker. John Archer wandered in, and a quick drink soon

The poverty in the city gave rise to a criminal underclass. Prostitution and robbery were rife. Author's collection

A fool and his money.... Strand Magazine

became a couple, and then a few more. By 8 o'clock he was rather the worse for wear and had been noticed by a couple of the girls, Esther Bates and one of her friends. They watched him sitting alone downing drinks for a while and decided to make the most of it.

John finally stood up and staggered out of the pub. Esther and her friend followed him out and found him leaning heavily against a wall. A bit of banter was quickly succeeded by each of them grabbing an arm and marching him off to Esther's house just around the corner. John protested, but not sufficiently convincingly or strenuously. Within a few minutes they had hustled him through the door and locked it behind them.

John complained and tried to get out of the room. Esther grabbed his hat and ran off up the stairs with it, taunting him. John managed to get up the stairs after her. She told him that since he was in a brothel the only way he could have his hat back was if he did some business. The newspaper accounts of the time draw a polite veil over the ensuing few minutes, which concluded with John Archer paying Esther Bates two shillings. The trouble was he now discovered she had pinched the entire seventeen shillings he had made earlier. He was not best impressed and demanded she give the money back. Esther Bates had no intention of doing any such thing, threatening to throw him down the stairs and emphasised this with a punch to his chest.

Downstairs was Ann Sanders and another client by the name of Pemberton. Ann raced to the door to make sure it was locked as John came down saying he was going to call the Watch. As John struggled with the bolts and locks Ann ran to the fireplace and picked up a heavy poker and started to belt him over the head with it. He collapsed under the rain of blows. Pemberton made himself as inconspicuous as he could. Esther was shrieking for help, and another girl, Maria Birchley, came out of one of the rooms. She took one look at Esther, pretending to collapse fainting into a chair, and saw Ann cracking John Archer over the head with a poker. She grabbed the nearest weapon to hand, a pair of candlesnuffers, and shoved it into the poor man's ear.

Maria Birchley said she would go out and get the watch to arrest Archer, but she soon returned, not with the law, but a trio of local villains: William Worrall, William Hudson and Oliver Turner. They started pushing John around and demanding to know what was going on. He called for the Watch repeatedly but Turner just laughed, saying:

'You shall have a clock, and I'll wind it up for you.'

The gang pounced and started punching him. In the confusion John Archer managed to get out of the door and stumble into the street. The trouble was he had no idea where to run and soon ended in a dead end. Hudson and another rogue called Jones dragged him back into the house.

Ann Sanders had pulled all the chairs out of the way and as John Archer was hauled back into the dingy room, she rolled up her sleeves and said she would have the first go at the b****, claiming that this was a woman's cause and they would finish it. By now they had all convinced themselves that John had defrauded them. The fact Esther had stolen all his money was conveniently forgotten.

The men called out of the pub for a scrap, thought this was unfair. They wanted to stick the boot in too. John Archer, battered and bruised, had to listen to an almighty argument about whether the men or the women should finish him off. Unfortunately for him they came to a compromise; they all descended on him and beat him out of the house and into the yard behind. John Archer was now begging for his life, imploring them not to kill him and saying they should take him to the watch house if they thought he had wronged them. Someone, probably Sanders, smashed a poker into the back of his head, and Oliver Turner punched him to the ground, grabbing his throat to stifle his cries for help. Darkness enveloped John Archer.

John drifted back to consciousness after spending fifteen hours in oblivion. He was paralysed from the waist down and covered in massive bruising. He had been discovered in the road and taken into the *Kings Head*. Here he hovered on the edge of life, so ill that they dared not move him for fifteen weeks. A little recovered, he was taken home to Alcester and the prosecution started of the wicked gang that had so abused him. Everyone except Oliver Turner was arrested within days of the attack. They were thrown into one of the dank cells of Warwick Gaol and awaited their trial with despair, charged with attempted murder, a capital offence.

John Archer was still hovering between life and death when the next assizes took place that summer. By the autumn assizes he was slightly recovered but nowhere near strong enough to give evidence and it wasn't until the spring of 1823 that he was considered just about capable of giving his evidence. He was carried into the courtroom on a stretcher, still unable to move his legs. The stretcher was placed on a table so that people could see him, but his voice was so weak and quiet that few could hear what he said. An assistant repeated his words in a louder voice. His evidence was consistent, and damning for the three women and four men in the dock. Pemberton was accused of failing to assist him in his moment of need, but he said that he would have suffered exactly the same fate if he had dared to intervene. However, he gave evidence that agreed entirely with John Archer's story. The defence asked a few desultory questions but this seemed to do little more than harden the jury against them. Even though they all denied the murderous attack they were found guilty of the assault and sentenced to eighteen months' hard labour. This was in addition to the year in which they had been held in the gaol.

The local paper described the incident as one of 'unparalleled brutality' and a stern warning to all those readers, especially the young, to avoid visiting the haunts of infamy and vice. A sentiment as true today as it was then.

It probably won't come as a surprise to discover that this was just one of hundreds of similar incidents involving the brothels of Birmingham. Sarah Ann Jones was charged with highway robbery with violence in December 1860. Ah ha, I thought as I trawled through the old newspapers, could be a good case involving black masks, magnificent horses jumping seven foot turnpike gates and three-cornered hats. But in 1860 the turnpikes were a shadow of their former glory, canals and railways took passengers in much greater comfort and safety. The toll collectors on the turnpikes were busy tending their allotments and had left the gates open. So how on earth did Sarah Ann Jones manage to get done for Highway robbery? Well it's very familiar story.

Michael Finnigan had done a pretty good days business in the Birmingham market. He had earned £64, which was a substantial sum (in today's terms it is the equivalent of £4,100). He felt he deserved a drink, and so popped into a pub in Vale Street. It was one of those sorts of pubs. Sarah Ann wandered up to him and asked if he would like to treat her. Indeed he did, and bought several rounds of drinks. After a while the somewhat tipsy and cheerful Michael Finnigan was led gently out of the pub and round the corner to a brothel. Once they got inside Michael asked one of the girls if she could pop over to the pub and get a flagon of beer to liven up the fun.

When the girl returned with the beer she rather spoilt things by trying to cut off his pocket with the money in. He wasn't impressed. All his amorous plans for Sarah Ann evaporated and he suddenly felt that she had lured him into a den of thieves. She had. He struggled back into his coat and lurched out of the front door, swaying after all the beer. He tried to see what the house number was, but it was all a bit blurred. He set off down the road.

Sarah Ann had no intention of watching £64 leave her life so suddenly. She followed him out of the door and down the street. Seeing one of her friends, she gestured to him across the road to stop Michael. Her friend was probably not one you would want to meet on a dark night, in fact lunchtime wasn't such a good idea for Michael. He was knocked to the ground by one almighty blow to the head. As he lay stunned in the dirty gutter,

Vale Street was one of the more dubious areas of the city.

Strand Magazine

Sarah Ann jumped on him and used a knife to cut off the pocket with all his money in. She vanished into the crowds along with her accomplice.

When Michael recovered he went to the police. In 1860 this was a comparatively unusual thing to do. Most people who were robbed by prostitutes were far too ashamed to admit that they went anyway near a brothel, but £64 was a fortune. Inspector Tandy took him back to the street and got him to point out which was the house. He wasn't surprised to find which one it was. After a few days Sarah Ann was arrested, although her friend who had knocked Michael down escaped detection.

Sarah Ann Jones was sentenced to six years in prison. She tried to say that it was the other girl who had followed him out of the house, but Michael was adamant in his identification of her. Inspector Tandy added that the house was one of the most notorious in the whole of Birmingham and that the money that had been stolen there was simply unbelievable.

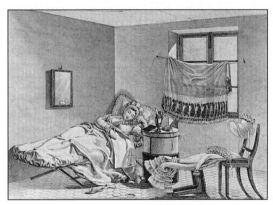

What was waiting inside a brothel was not always what was expected.
Strand Magazine

CHAPTER 3

Mary Ann Higgins

COVENTRY

1831

*He went out to the privvy in the yard
and was very sick.*

L ife at the start of the nineteenth century could be pretty rough. Mary Ann Higgins was born in the small market town of Henley in Arden in 1812. The town was one of the many agricultural markets serving the needs of the growing cities like Birmingham. Mary's mother had married into the Higgins family, who were from Coventry. For some reason, we'll never know why, Mary's mother completely rejected her child and by the time her baby was a year old, she had persuaded her in-laws to take the little

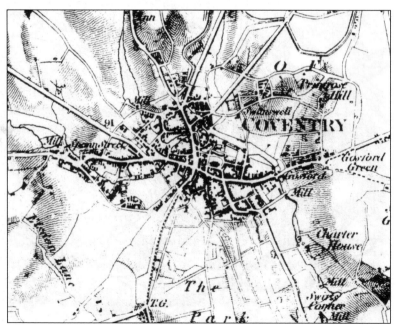

Victorian Coventry. Author's collection

Mary and raise her in their family home in Coventry. She stayed on in Henley and had plenty of other children, so her rejection of this child seems to be something of a mystery.

Her grandparents in Coventry raised Mary Ann for the next ten years. Unfortunately, as was so often the case in those days, they died. The average life expectancy was about forty-five for most city dwellers, even less in places like Birmingham or Liverpool. Mary Ann was left effectively orphaned. She tried to go back to her mother's home in Henley, but was rejected once again. There was one relative who offered her a home, an aunt in Manchester, and so Mary Ann made the long journey to the north of England at just thirteen years old.

There was a catch, there usually is. Mary's aunt ran a brothel. By the time she was fourteen she was paying for her keep by working as a prostitute. Presumably she earnt a fair bit of money, young pretty girls always attracted the rich clients. Mary began to acquire a taste for fine clothes and the high life.

Spon Street, Coventry, some of the oldest surviving buildings in the city. Unfortunately we don't know which was the Higgins household. The author

For the next few years Mary seemed quite at home in the brothel, but fate was only bidding its time. Her aunt died in 1827 and the brothel collapsed. Mary Ann was once again cut adrift and had to seek employment as a domestic maid.

Life as a maid didn't suit the now worldly-wise and free spending Mary Ann. The wages were meagre and it wasn't long before she was caught pilfering money and clothes from her new employers. She moved from job to job around Manchester, narrowly escaping prosecution for theft several times. It was time to move on once again. She still had an uncle in Coventry, and so at the age of eighteen she moved back down south, at Michaelmas 1830, settling with her bachelor uncle, Mr William Higgins.

William Higgins lived in Spon Street, Coventry. He seems to have been in his mid-forties and had spent most of his life working as a labourer on the farm of John Moore. Although this might seem to be a fairly humble occupation, William was surprisingly wealthy. He had inherited money, and saved plenty as well. All in all he had £113 saved in an account administered by John Moore. It was a substantial amount for the period, about £7,800 in modern times. His house in Spon Street wasn't a particularly large one, with four rooms fronting onto the street and a shared courtyard at the back. The houses in Spon Street were all very old and dilapidated, nothing like the new modern buildings that were being built on the edge of the city.

Mary settled into life with her uncle through the winter of 1830 quite happily. He seemed to be fond of her and most of the neighbours thought that she was just as fond of him. Mary soon found herself a boyfriend, one Edward Clarke. She was now 19 and he was 27. Edward soon realised that Mary could get her hands on some of her uncle's money and would persuade her to pilfer a bit of cash every now and then. It was small change in comparison to what Mary was pinching for her own use.

By March Mary was well known to John Wilson, a brewer further down the road. She would regularly come into his premises to buy ale to take home, and quite often she would ask for change for a sovereign. John suggested she was spending her fortune rather too quickly. She showed him a ring on her finger and said she was to be married at Easter. Edward Clarke had

You could buy all sorts of toxic chemicals quite freely if you had a witness to back up your claim to need them. The author

proposed to her at long last.

History does not reveal much detail about the relationship between Mary Ann Higgins and Edward Clarke. He was older than her, but she had clearly led a far more experienced life. She was fond enough of him to give him substantial quantities of money, even if it wasn't hers to give. He had proposed to her, and it seems this was very much against the wishes of William Higgins, or 'old wart head' as Edward called him to his friends. Edward worked at Vale & Co and his workmates often commented on how he was getting money from Mary. Naturally once it all went horribly wrong, accusations were flying around everywhere. As things stood in March 1831, Mary Ann Higgins was to be the sole inheritor of William Higgins' money, and once she married Edward Clarke, that money would become his.

On the morning of 22 March Mary went out shopping. Her first port of call was the druggists further down Spon Street. She asked James Jenson for a pennyworth of arsenic. There were a couple of problems. He only sold it in two pennyworth packets and she did not have a witness with her. In those days you could easily buy poisons for killing off rats and mice, but you did need to have a witness to back up your claim to be buying it for a legitimate purpose. Somewhat thwarted, Mary left. Next she visited Messers Stott and Wiley, another druggists. Here she asked for a two penny pack of arsenic and was once again told that she needed a witness. Mary said she was from the country and so didn't know many people in town. Then she said she had a sister and would come back in a while.

Mary Ann wandered off past the barracks until she bumped into Elizabeth Russell. She explained to her that she needed to buy some arsenic to kill off the rats and persuaded her to come back to Stott & Wiley's. John Wiley, the apprentice, now had no problem in serving her. He wrapped up the arsenic in two paper wrappers and stuck a label on it: Arsenic, Poison. Mary asked him how to use the poison and he gave her a recipe for a rat bait. Once out in the street Elizabeth was surprised to see Mary Ann pull off the label and throw it away, saying: 'I wonder why they put that on it?'

Shopping complete, Mary went over to Messers Rotherham & Vale to meet Edward Clarke. Thomas Smith and Edward Pearson watched the two of them walking towards Spon End on the way back to her house. The young couple went into the house.

William Higgins left work around quarter past six that evening. He was in good health and quite happy when he said good night to John Moore and John Patrick on the farm. He got back to the house in Spon Street and sat down to supper with

Mary Ann and Edward Clarke. It was pea soup, William preferred his soup thickened with flour, whilst Mary and Edward had theirs thickened with oatmeal. This made William's soup look quite white, whilst theirs was a yellow colour. Another reason was that Mary had emptied the packet of arsenic into his bowl before pouring the soup into it.

Arsenic is a tasteless compound and was widely believed to be untraceable at the time. However, like most poisons, it has to be administered in the correct dosage to be really effective. Too little and your victim gets poorly but recovers, too much and they are violently sick and expel the toxin from their system before it does any lasting damage. Mary had put far too much into the soup bowl, but she hadn't stirred it up. William tucked into his soup, but didn't finish it all. The next few hours would tell if he would live or die. Feeling a bit off colour, he went to have a lie down.

After supper Mary put the unfinished bowls of soup into the pantry and casually sat chatting with Edward until nine. That was the time that William would normally go to the privy and then retire for the night. William now had a terrible headache and his back was aching. He went out to the privy in the yard and was very sick. Catherine Dutton, who lived next door, heard his familiar footsteps, and also heard him being sick, but didn't realise the gravity of the situation. William went back upstairs to bed, groaning in pain. Edward Clarke called up to him to see if he wanted anything to drink, but the old man refused. Edward then asked if he wanted a doctor, but Mary told him that nothing would do him any good now. Edward asked again if he wanted a doctor and was about to go out and get one when Mary pulled him back by the coat tails. Edward took him up a cup of tea and then went home. Elizabeth Dalton the housekeeper for Mr Samuel Spilman in the house directly across the road had watched Mary and Edward saying good night. She had also seen old Mr Higgins struggling back into the house from the privy wiping his mouth with a napkin as though he had just been sick again.

Once William Higgins retired in agony to his bed upstairs, it seems that Mary Ann started to search the house for any money lying around, turning over cushions and opening cupboards. Although most of William's money was tied up in an account that she would eventually get her hands on, a little spending money wouldn't go amiss at this juncture. If nothing else there would be a funeral to pay for very soon. Upstairs, William's groans of agony gradually subsided.

The thin walls of the houses carried his groans through them with comparative ease. Next-door, Elizabeth Welch was woken by the sound and looked out. Mary's window was lit with a candle and she could hear her walking about the house. Someone, she wasn't sure who, was muttering: 'Oh Dear, Oh dear'. It was about midnight.

At around two in the morning Mary Ann Higgins went twenty odd yards down the road to Ellen Green's house and banged on the door. 'Mrs Green, will you get up, my uncle is very bad.' Ellen had known William for many years and been his neighbour for at least five years. Despite this, she was feeling ill that night and couldn't get herself dressed. She called out for Mary to find someone else. About ten minutes later Mary was back, banging on the door insistently, and said: 'Mrs Green, God bless you, get up, for I think my uncle is dying.'

Ellen Green struggled into her clothes and went round to the house. She found William lying partly on his side leaning over the bed as though he had been sick. She shook him and called: 'William, William', but he didn't respond. She went downstairs to the kitchen to brew up some tea, leaving Mary Ann upstairs. As she was blowing the fire back into life Mary Ann came down and said: 'Lord, my uncle has just given such a groan, did you not hear it?' Ellen rushed back upstairs and shook William again, but he never stirred. He was cold and stiff, Ellen judged that he had been dead half an hour. 'Oh, dear, dear, why did you not send for someone before?' Mary replied: 'Because I was in bed and asleep and so did not hear him.' Ellen offered to go and get some more people, but Mary would not hear of it.

Mrs Chambers arrived and they went back up to the Mary's room, for that was where William lay. Mary explained that she had dragged him into her bed when she realised he was ill. 'Oh my dear uncle, my dear uncle is gone, all my friends are gone' and Mary broke down in tears loud enough for the entire street to hear.

Ellen Green managed to get away for fifteen minutes now that Mrs Chambers had arrived. The news was soon all over the city centre. Ellen returned and sat in the kitchen with Mary Ann talking about this and that. Mary told her that she was due to get married at Easter, and it would be an 'all-in-one' wedding since she was in the family way. She also told her that although William had not made a proper will, he had said in front of two witnesses that he wanted to leave all his worldly goods to her. Mrs Parker and John Low would vouch that everything was now hers. With that in mind Mary gave her a bundle of sheets and other oddments to keep safe, ostensibly because she was young and foolish and might lose some of the things in the house. Ellen Green took the things with her when she went home to get some breakfast at seven.

By now the whole street was aware that William Higgins had died suddenly in the night. Elizabeth Moore from Hill Street arrived at about ten and the house was bustling with activity. Mrs Green was back again, as were Elizabeth Welch, William Webb and a few others. Mary was putting on a black dress and getting ready to go out with Mrs Southam to organise the mourning. Elizabeth Moore stayed in the house and started to tidy things up, it was all very untidy, as though someone had ransacked it. She tidied the parlour and then went into the kitchen. When she opened the pantry she saw two bowls of pea soup, one of which looked very odd indeed, an unhealthy shade of white, and most unlike ordinary pea soup. She put the bowls back where she found them and wondered what she should do. She wasn't sure that she could trust Welch or Webb. At about twelve Thomas Minstrell, the carpenter, arrived. He had already been summoned to measure the old man for his coffin. Here at least was someone that Mrs Moore felt she could trust, and she took the bowls of soup up to him as he worked in the bedroom upstairs. He noticed the strange colour and peculiar thickness of the one bowl and decided to put them in the room with the corpse.

At much the same time Mr William Hume and Mr William Barton arrived. They were two local surgeons who had been instructed to investigate the death by the Chief Constable, Mr Barton. The rumours had flown around the whole city by now. Matters were probably not helped by Edward Clarke who had turned up at the house briefly at about seven and then gone into work and happily announced that 'old wart head is dead.'

Edward Baker, one of the apprentices, thought it was in bad taste, but Edward told him he was going to be married and the old man was worth some money and had decked him out for the wedding.

The surgeons took samples of the contents of the old man's stomach and set about testing these, and the dubious looking soup. News that Mary had bought some arsenic the previous day also got around. It didn't take a complete genius to work out what had happened and Thomas Gardner the local constable was instructed to arrest Mary Ann that evening. The first tests for arsenic were positive, both in the soup and in the old man. They saved the soup for further testing on a rather unlucky dog. The dog took a small amount of the soup and was instantly sick. It survived as a result of this sudden reaction. Although the general public believed that arsenic could not be traced this was not the case. The science of chemistry was making great strides forward and a process using silver nitrate could reveal the presence of arsenic straight away. This gave the surgeons their first indication of the poison. They went on to conduct further tests by filtering and boiling down the soup over the next few days and extracted the actual arsenic itself.

Of course even back in 1831 when someone was arrested they were supposed to be warned that anything they said may used in evidence against them. Officially anyway.

Thomas Gardner went round to the Spon Street and arrested Mary Ann. When she asked him why, he told her it was for the poisoning of William Higgins. She protested that she had done no such thing. Constable Gardner insisted that she walk with him back to his house where she would be held in custody. Before they set off he asked her if she had bought the poison and she denied. He then told her that he could bring Miss Russell to prove that she had. Mary Ann then remembered that she had and pointed to a dead mouse. Thomas collected the dead mouse as possible evidence. He then searched her. The search revealed over nine guineas in various pockets of her dress.

As they were walking down the street he asked her if she had been persuaded by anyone to do the deed. She told him that no one had persuaded her. He then asked her what made her do it. She told him that she had had a row with her uncle about the wedding. He continued to pump her for information about the incident and eventually got her to admit that she had put two teaspoons of arsenic in the bowl of soup. Once they got back to the watch house he managed to get her to repeat the confession in front of four other people. Then he mentioned that she should not say anything that might incriminate her in the deed.

The coroner played his part somewhat more legally a couple of days later. Both Mary Ann and Edward Clark were arrested for the felonious administering of poison to William. Edward was also charged with a secondary charge of aiding and abetting a murder. The mouse that Mary Ann had said had been poisoned with the arsenic turned out to have died of natural causes, it contained no poison at all. The poison had been solely intended for the old man.

EXECUTION AT COVENTRY.—On Thursday the awful sentence of the law was carried into effect on *Mary Ann Higgins*, convicted of the murder of her uncle, William Higgins, of that city. During her imprisonment she had been impressed with a conviction that the evidence to be produced against her was such as to leave no hope of acquittal; and yet her conduct up to the time of her trial was such as amounted to absolute levity. She frequently asserted that her fellow prisoner, *Clarke*, participated in the murder, and that it was done by his instigation. After her condemnation, however, she appeared reconciled to her fate.

Warwickshire Advertiser

The case came before Warwick Assizes on 9 August. The case ran from nine in the morning through to eight that night. There wasn't much doubt about Mary Ann's part in the killing, but the role of Edward Clarke was something of a mystery. Did he know anything about the poison or not? After listening to a long defence, and quite a few character witnesses the judge advised the jury that he almost certainly was not guilty of both charges. In her defence Mary Ann then blamed him for the whole affair saying on oath that he had started off bullying her to give him money, and this had escalated to physical violence.

Eventually he came up with the plan to do away with the old man, and if she didn't follow his plan then he would kill her. Neither the judge nor jury were convinced by this defence and when they retired to consider their verdict they were only gone a few minutes. They returned to pronounce Mary Ann Higgins guilty of murder, and Edward Clarke not guilty of both charges. Mary made no comment. Indeed her behaviour throughout the trial had been flippant on the verge of contempt. Now that the judge donned his black cap the awful import of what had happened finally sank in and as he read the death sentence she broke down in tears.

The Honourable Sir Joseph Littledale told her that her time left on earth was limited, and he really wasn't joking. The execution was set for 18 August. Her mother and sister visited her on the day before her execution. It may have been a strained meeting considering that this was the mother whose rejection

Tranquil enough today, Whitley Common was the traditional place for executions in the early nineteenth century. The author

had left her to slide down into a life of prostitution and theft. That evening Mary Ann asked the female warder to read to her until she fell asleep. She awoke at four on the fateful day and received the last rites. Her mother came back one last time to bid her farewell. Outside the gaol a cart waited. The under sheriff of the county and some of his officers escorted her to the cart and she clambered into the back and sat on her own coffin. The cart set off towards Whitley Common, followed by the executioner, a priest and many thousands of people. It took half an hour to reach the site on the common where the scaffold had been erected. There were between 15,000 and 20,000 people milling around. The sheriff's officers formed a circle around the scaffold and pushed the vast milling crowd out to a distance of forty feet. Mary Ann Higgins ascended the scaffold with a firm step. The executioner removed her bonnet, and placed a cap over her head that concealed her face, he then pinioned her arms to her sides and loosely tied her ankles together. He then placed a white handkerchief in her hand and climbed down the scaffold. The handkerchief was to be his signal, after a few moments she dropped the handkerchief and he pulled the trap from under her. She dropped to her death.

As was the practise in those days, after her body had hung for an hour it was cut down and conveyed to the local doctors for dissection. They hoped that their new insights into anatomy would in some way make up for the damage Mary Ann had caused by poisoning her uncle. They were already pretty good at detecting arsenic. The Coventry constable, Thomas Gardner, was severely criticised both during and after the trial for interrogating Mary Ann before reading her her rights. However, his evidence was allowed and her confession was the principal evidence used to condemn her.

Public opinion was that Mary Ann Higgins had been led away from the path of virtue by pride and a fondness for dresses. Right to the end Mary Ann continued to say that she had been led astray by Edward Clarke and that it was all his idea.

CHAPTER 4

Susannah Perry

ROWLEY REGIS

1838

*As she entered the room he gave one huge
sigh and expired.*

The genesis of my crime books started during researches into my family history and the discovery of the murder of my great great grandfather. One branch of the Billingham brood comes from the area around Cradley Heath and Rowley Regis where they were chain and nailmakers. While I was hunting down snippets of information about the antics of my ancestors, I came across this little insight into life as a nailmaker – and death too. It might not be in Warwickshire, but it's part of my family folklore so vaguely relevant.

Samuel and Susannah Perry lived in Garretts Lane, Rowley Regis in 1838. Samuel was a nailor, a nailmaker. He would spend his days in a workshop at the back of the house turning iron wire into heavy nails. It was hot, hard and heavy work, but he earnt just enough money for him to support his wife and their three children. He was forty-five years old and in good health. It wouldn't be uncommon for him to work twelve hours a day for six days of every week. Holidays were pretty much unknown in those days and life in the Black Country could be unremittingly hard.

Susannah not only had the children to raise but also worked at home weaving straw bonnets for a few extra pennies. Generally life was all hard work and no play. The house was crowded. Not only were there Samuel and Susannah and their three children, but Samuel's two sisters also lived with them.

Susannah did manage to find a little extra entertainment though, in the form of a younger man by the name of Smith. It was soon the gossip of the neighbourhood. John Embury worked with Smith in one of the many coal mines in the district and often teased him about it.

A nailmaker's workshop at the Black Country Museum. The author

At the start of July matters started to take a more sinister turn. No one thought anything of it at the time, but one of Susannah's close friends bought some arsenic from a local druggist. By the end of the first week of July Samuel was starting to feel ill in the mornings.

On Wednesday 10 July, Samuel got up early and went down to his workshop. At half-five in the morning John Embury was making his way to work and noticed him hammering away at his nailmaking iron. He also noticed that Susannah was in the garden, leaning over the hedge whispering something to Smith, who was standing in the lane. Their heads were very close together but he couldn't quite see if they were kissing.

Samuel worked on through the morning. He hadn't bothered with breakfast since his stomach was upset and when Susannah came to see him at dinner time he just asked for a quartern of brandy and a quartern of gin. By mid-afternoon he was dreadfully ill, retching and sweating. Susannah put him to bed and went to get his mother.

Rachel Perry arrived at about one o'clock. Samuel was in a dreadful state and she sat with him through the afternoon and evening. Rachel suggested getting a doctor but Samuel was having none of it.

'No doctor for me, mother, the Lord will be my doctor and friend.'

Doctors in 1838 were staggeringly expensive, and for the most part utterly useless, so Samuel's refusal to send for one is not that surprising.

Strand Magazine

Sarah Baker, who lived next door, also came round to help. There wasn't a great deal to be done though. Samuel was adamant that they shouldn't get him a doctor. He managed to drink some brandy and some buck bean tea, but that didn't help him improve at all. Rachel Perry and Sarah Baker left the house late that evening. Smith also popped in to see how Samuel was.

At one the following morning, Sarah was woken by Susannah rattling the door.

'Sarah, do get up, for our Samuel is dying.'

Sarah rushed round and went into the bedroom. Samuel was lying half dressed across the bed. As she entered the room he gave one huge sigh and expired. By dawn the house was in an uproar. Word had gone around and another word had come straight back. Sarah told her about the rumour that she had poisoned Samuel. Susannah told Sarah that she was innocent and had never done anything to hurt Samuel.

Samuel's body was laid out on the bed during the Thursday and who should arrive first thing on Friday morning but Constable James Detheridge. He wanted to know if there was any truth in the rumours that were flying around. One of the first things he wanted to know was why a doctor had not been called, and he wasn't very happy to be told by Susannah that Samuel hadn't wanted one. Constable Detheridge told her not

Strand Magazine

to move the body, and that he would return with a surgeon the following day to hold an inquest. Susannah went up the wall and objected long and loud. It was a natural death, no good would come of an autopsy, they should leave her alone with her grief. The constable was having none of it.

On Friday 13 August, Constable Detheridge returned together with Constable Jewkes of Dudley and Mr Fereday, the surgeon. Susannah was absolutely beside herself with worry and flung herself on to Samuel's cold corpse. She was insistent that no one should touch his body. The constables tried to reason with her, but nothing would persuade her to let go. Eventually they had to physically drag her off and lock her out of the room. She was alternating between hysterical screaming fits and fainting. Mr Fereday proceeded with the autopsy, paying particular attention to the contents of Samuel's stomach. The two constables decided to search the house rather than watch the gruesome examination.

As they were checking through the kitchen Constable Jewkes found a blue paper packet containing some powder. It appeared to have come from Mr Lawton's druggists. They decided to get the contents analysed. The autopsy took over four hours and by the end of it things were looking decidedly bleak for Susannah Perry.

The results of the autopsy and chemical tests came through

by the next week. The blue paper packet contained arsenic, as did the contents of Samuel's stomach. Susannah Perry was arrested and charged with the wilful murder of her husband. There were some complicating factors though. The friend of Susannah's that had purchased the poison had vanished and so could not give evidence. Smith too failed to give evidence at the inquest. It could have easily been Smith that poisoned Samuel, he had the opportunity and quite certainly the motive. Susannah's behaviour when the surgeon came to do the autopsy suggests that she knew she would be implicated in murder, but not necessarily that she was the one that had done it. The case appears to have gone cold after the coroner's inquest and no trial was subsequently reported.

Poisonings can take a variety of guises. The old arsenic in the dinner being the most common; but I came across a most peculiar case in 1850. It quite flummoxed the jury at the time and still remains a puzzle to this day.

A typically dire kitchen of the squalid back-to-back cottages. The author

MURDER OF A HUSBAND.

An inquiry, which occasioned intense excitement at Rowley-Regis and its neighbourhood, has occupied the earnest attention of Mr. Smith, and an intelligent coroner's jury, for several days in the course of the last three weeks. Samuel Perry, a nailor, living in Garrett's-lane, it was reported, had been poisoned by his wife, and the object of the investigation was to ascertain the truth of this horrible charge. The facts of the case (which is not quite free from mystery, in consequence of the constable being unable to find a girl who could, most likely, have given important testimony) will be gathered from the accompanying abstract of the evidence :—

Warwickshire Advertiser

Bridget Tameney was twenty-three in 1849. She was a single mother who lived in Warwick. There was no question about the care and affection that she lavished on her first child, even if being a single mother in Victorian society was deeply disgraceful. For working-class people marriage was frequently an option that was simply too expensive and casual liaisons were by no means uncommon. Bridget was fairly typical, she could barely read or write and had virtually no education. Not surprisingly perhaps, she became pregnant again and towards Christmas was admitted to the workhouse. This was the only effective form of health care for the poor. The workhouse provided the very basic needs, food and shelter, together with rudimentary medical care. There was a special ward for maternity care and it was in this was that Bridget gave birth to a baby boy on 27 December 1849. She had been in the ward for a couple weeks beforehand and the nurse, Hannah Walters said both mother and baby were perfectly healthy.

This was all to change a couple of days later. On Saturday morning, Hannah noticed that the baby was listless and his lips had gone blue. She called in the master of the workhouse, Mr Hilton. The baby continued to worsen and the local surgeon was called in the afternoon. Mr Blenkinsop looked at the child but couldn't quite fathom what the blue colour around the baby's lips and mouth was. After he left, Hannah went to see how Bridget and the baby were getting on. The baby was even worse, and Bridget was worried sick about the little mite. Hannah found what appeared to be some blue stones or crystals on the bed and also on the floor. She then found a small box of the same crystals. She took them straight to Mr Hilton.

'How came you to administer such stuff to your infant?' he asked Bridget.

'I gave it to my infant to do it good.'

'How did you come by it?'

'It was given to me by a Mrs Green, a navvie's wife, who lived in the Saltisford.'

Mr Hilton told her that the crystals were copper sulphate, and poisonous.

'I am very sorry for what I have done. I hope the child won't die and I hope if I get over this trouble I shall be more careful for the future.'

Mr Blenkinsop was called back to examine the baby again. But there was no antidote that he knew of. When he asked Bridget where she had got the crystals from she gave him a rather evasive reply, which annoyed him intensely. A baby's life was at stake and he didn't have the time to mess around.

Through the Saturday night and on into the Sunday the baby slowly weakened and eventually it died at eight on the Sunday morning. Bridget Tameneh was charged with the wilful murder of her child and sent to Warwick Gaol.

Bridget was brought to trial in April. Despite repeated searches, the mysterious Mrs Green could not be found. Was she a real person who had been so malicious as to persuade Bridget to administer a poison to her child or was she a figment of Bridget's imagination and a fiction to get her off the charge of murder? After a long discussion the jury decided that Bridget's account was true and that the charge of murder should be thrown out. However, that still left the charge of manslaughter, and they found her guilty of that. They did however recommend the judge to mercy, on the grounds that Bridget was of limited intelligence and did not understand the danger of administering an unknown chemical to her child. The judge accepted their advice and sentenced her to just six months in prison.

Mrs Green was never found. Perhaps she derived some perverted satisfaction at killing a child by proxy, or perhaps she was just stupid and superstitious, quite unaware that the Blue Vitriol would kill a baby in tiny doses.

CHAPTER 5

Elizabeth Varney and Hannah Smith
LEAMINGTON SPA
1840

It wasn't long before they pulled out not just one drowned girl, but two.

The newspapers of Warwickshire for the nineteenth century are full of various tales of murder and mayhem. Not all the violence is directed at someone else though; surprisingly often the fury and frustration turns inward and results in suicide. When I was researching my first book about crimes I discovered the stark numbers of suicides in Edwardian Birmingham. For many women revenge against an abusive husband was impossible and they vented their anger and despair on themselves. Navigating boats along the Birmingham canals must have required a strong stomach; they offered a quick escape from an impossible life to hundreds of Birmingham women. There were times during the research when I wondered how they managed to find an empty bit to jump into. They must have been queuing at the bridges.

The people of Leamington Spa were shocked to the core at the start of July 1840 by a remarkable event. At twenty to five on the morning of Wednesday 1 July, John Smith was on the way to his job as a porter. As he was passing Mr Oldham's mill by the river he noticed a bonnet lying on the dam. On approaching it he noticed there was a shawl folded up beneath it, and that there was another bonnet and shawl next to it, with a letter beside it. Somewhat concerned John called at the mill and asked the miller what should be done. The miller suggested that he should go straight to the police. John Smith gathered up the bonnets, shawls and letter and walked over to the constable's house.

Constable Roby looked at the letter; it was a suicide note. He hurried back to the mill dam with John Smith, and persuaded John Harris to help drag the mill pool. It wasn't long before they pulled out not just one drowned girl, but two. They carried the

The site of the old mill, now beneath the ornamental lake
in the Jefferson Gardens. The author

bodies over to the Newbold Inn and called for a surgeon to ascertain the cause of their deaths.

Ralph Augustus Busby, the surgeon, arrived at the inn by half five. He soon concluded that both girls had died by drowning and had been in the water for at least an hour. The local coroner, Mr G C Greenway, called an inquest for the following day to try to discover what had made to young women do away with themselves.

By the time of the inquest rumour and gossip had swept through the whole town and most of the protagonists of the affair were ready to give their statements. The two girls were Elizabeth Varney and Hannah Smith. Both had been crossed in love and they had not known each other until just a few days before their suicide pact. Elizabeth had married a soldier, but he had dumped her and run off in the spring of 1840. Elizabeth, who was just twenty-one, was too proud to go back to her parents. She managed to find lodgings with Jane Crump at 21 Oxford Street. She took two rooms explaining that they were for both her and her husband. Elizabeth hadn't wasted much time in finding a previous boyfriend, William Southam and moving him in. Jane Crump was under the impression that he was her husband.

William was just a year older than Elizabeth and worked as a cart driver for Mr Colledge. Within days the gossip was out that he was going around to Elizabeth's every night. After a week Mr Colledge took William off to one side and explained that his conduct was out of order and he should wait until he could marry her and be a good Christian. Just to make sure that he got the message, Mr Colledge told him that he would get the sack if he didn't break off his relationship with Elizabeth. A few days later Jane Crump was told about the improper goings on and that she was in danger of running a house of ill-repute. Elizabeth and William were promptly given notice to quit.

In another house in Leamington a young servant girl, Hannah Smith, cried herself to sleep every night. She had worked for Mrs Ward since March and always seemed cheerful enough, partly because she was busy thinking about her boyfriend George Johnson, the tailor from Long Itchington. They had been lovers since she was fifteen. This all ended in the middle of June when he dumped her, and her world fell to pieces. Her friend Eliza Willias tried to comfort her, but with little effect. She was inconsolable and started to talk about killing herself. She wrapped up her best dresses and told Eliza to give them to Miss Burman.

On 30 June, a Tuesday, William Southam had already quit the lodgings, having given Elizabeth eight shillings to tide her over. He had made his choice between her and his job, and chosen the job. Elizabeth may already have met Hannah by now, she had had several other women visit her. She left the Oxford Street house at nine in the evening and walked into town and met up with the heartbroken Hannah. In town the two of them met George Whorrall and Elizabeth asked him to go into Mr Coate's Tap Room and ask William to come out and speak to her. George went in and saw William, saying that Elizabeth was outside and wanted to talk to him. William was certain of his decision now, and told George that he couldn't. He had given her enough money to get by on, and he really didn't dare lose his job. George went back out into the street and told Elizabeth that William wasn't going to come out. Crestfallen, Elizabeth suddenly went in and asked for a tea-cup, which the barman duly gave her.

Elizabeth and Hannah, together with George Whorrall walked down Guy Street, Elizabeth carefully holding the tea cup in front of her. When they reached the bottom of the street and George turned to go another way he bid them good-night.

A strange cheerfulness overtook the two girls once they decided to commit suicide together.

Strand Magazine

'Goodnight, George, I shall drown myself tonight.'

Hannah's voice from behind her added: 'I shall do the same.'

George was confused, Elizabeth laughed as she spoke and seemed cheerful enough, but the meaning of her words were chillingly clear.

A quarter of an hour later William Wells, another servant, met the ill-fated pair in Clarendon Street. He knew both Hannah and Elizabeth. They briefly stopped to chat and Elizabeth asked him to fasten her gown. She was trembling and when he had done the awkward clip, told him that it would be the last time he would do it. The two girls walked off into the dark night, directly towards the mill.

That was the last time anyone saw them alive. Sometime during the dark cold night they both slipped off their shawls and bonnets and stepped into the lethal embrace of the river.

Nearly fifty years later, Leamington was stunned by another tragic suicide. This one came quite out of the blue. Mr and Mrs Topping lived at Lindisfarne on the Warwick New Road. It was a substantial household and they employed Annie Pearton as their domestic servant. By 1889 Annie had been with them for the best part of ten years and they trusted her completely. As a result when they went away that autumn, they left her in complete charge of the house, with the keys to everything. Rather rashly, this included the keys to the safe where all Mrs Topping's jewellery and Mr Topping's stash of silver was stored.

Although they thought that Annie Pearton was a thirty-seven-year-old spinster with no interest in men, Annie had an admirer who, once the coast was clear, came around to the house. This admirer kept his identity very secret; rumour had it that he was already married. He only came round in the afternoons, possibly because the Topping's had arranged for another woman to stay each night with Annie for added security. They really didn't want the place burgled.

Just before the Topping's were due back from their vacation Annie Pearton called the police. There had been a burglary and the safe robbed of a substantial amount of silver and all Mrs Topping's necklaces and rings. Inspector Parkinson of the Leamington Police was called into to investigate, and he wasn't at all happy about what he found. The robbery was clearly an

Warwick New Road was home to some of the wealthiest residents of Leamington.
The author

inside job. The doors couldn't have been forced the way that Annie said, and the safe couldn't have just fallen open like that. The inspector needed to find this secret admirer, but Annie wasn't telling him, just sticking to her rather dubious story of a burglary.

The Toppings arrived back to find their house burgled and their cook of ten years service under suspicion. Luckily the losses were insured and Mrs Topping told Annie that there would be no question of her ever being prosecuted for theft. She was forgiven. This wasn't much consolation to Annie, who was now about to be charged by Inspector Parkinson. She was deeply agitated and quite probably emotionally distressed by the fact that her admirer had not been to see her since the robbery. Through the week after the Topping's return Annie became worse and worse. The inspector was putting her under pressure to name the secret admirer.

On Monday 11 November the household was up early. Mr Topping had to journey to Penrith and Annie cooked his breakfast before he left. Mrs Topping lingered a while in bed and then rang the bell and asked Annie to bring her a jug of warm water to wash with. Annie went back downstairs and Mrs

SHOCKING SUICIDE OF A DOMESTIC SERVANT AT MILVERTON.

Early on Monday morning a painful feeling of regret was created in and around Leamington in consequence of the sudden and mysterious death of a domestic servant, named Annie Pearton, 37 years of age, who had for some time past been in service at Mrs. Topping's, Lindisfarne Villa, Warwick New Road. It appears that she rose early to prepare breakfast for her master, who had to make a journey to Penrith. Shortly after Mr. Topping had departed Mrs. Topping heard groans, and going to the deceased found her lying upon the floor, evidently in great suffering. The poor girl said, "Lord have mercy upon me!" and died. Pearton had been in the service of Mr. and Mrs. Topping for several years, and was

Warwickshire Advertiser

Topping washed and then crossed the landing to the dressing room. As she did so she heard a faint moaning from the kitchen. She rushed downstairs and found Annie lying on the kitchen floor moaning in agony. She asked her what was the matter. Annie replied: 'Lord have mercy on me. Let me die.'

Mrs Topping raced out into the street and begged the first person going past to get a cab and the police. By the time she had got back to the kitchen Annie Pearton had stopped breathing. It was all a bit sudden, as far as Mrs Topping knew, there was no poison in the house.

Doctor Smith and Inspector Parkinson arrived within a few minutes. It was far too late to do anything for Annie. There was a wrap of blue paper and a spoon on the kitchen dresser and these, together with the contents of her stomach, proved to contain Battle's Vermin Killer. At the inquest held at the *Coventry Arms* the following day Inspector Parkinson gave his evidence, suggesting that she took her own life rather than be forced to give away her mysterious lover and presumed robber that had taken the family's silver.

CHAPTER 6

Ann Wheatcroft

BIRMINGHAM

1848

*Sarah stood there horrified as she heard a sickening
thud and then a piercing scream from the boy.*

Life in the run down warrens of the city of
Birmingham was cruel enough before the added
element of human cruelty. In street after street of
back to back courtyards whole families eked out a
precarious existence hovering on the edge of destitution.
Despite the gruelling conditions most people helped each other
out and created real communities. It was in the case of German
Wheatcroft that that community spirit tried to save a young lad
from a life of misery.

George Wheatcroft was living in Bristol Street, Birmingham
in 1846. Some of his relatives in Derby had been looking after
his children from a previous marriage and had to send them
back. Two boys and a girl arrived in Birmingham and moved in
with him. It seems that George was single at the time and
looked after the children quite well. They were all fit and
healthy, the oldest boy was just seven and his brother and sister
a few years younger. George worked as a painter was very
rarely out of work, so he had little trouble affording enough
food for them, and after they arrived he moved to a slightly
larger lodgings in one of the courts of New Canal Street. These
lodgings even had a cellar.

George soon married Ann Jennings, although there was some
doubt as to the legality of their marriage, partly because of her
previous casual relationship with a Mr Jennings, and partly from
the lack of any paperwork. Nevertheless, Ann took the name
Wheatcroft and moved in with George in New Canal Street.
George was thirty-two and Ann a little older at thirty-six. Once
she moved in, the condition of the children started to worry the
neighbours. Jane Cheadle lived just down the road and

A lot of marriages were very casual indeed.
Strand Magazine

frequently saw Ann beat the boy German with clenched fists and sometimes with a heavy cane. She was utterly ruthless in her punishments of the child so much so that on several occasions both she and some of the other neighbours intervened.

Mrs Bland ran the local shop and was soon dismayed to see the way the little boy was treated. He wasn't allowed out very often, but whenever he came to the shop on his own Mrs Bland would give him a bit of bread or a snack. German would grab the food and devour it voraciously. He was starving. Mrs Bland saw the bruises on his skin and went around to the house to see what the matter was. There she found German with a rope tied to his leg, and the other end fastened to a heavy box. He was standing, holding a school book and apparently learning something. Ann was sitting at the table eating her tea. Mrs Bland asked how she could leave the lad so long without food or comfort.

'Look you, Mrs Bland, shouldn't you be ashamed to sit there three days learning a task; and he shan't have a bit nor sup until he can say it.'

Mrs Bland once again asked how she could keep him for so long without food and once again Ann told her that he would get nothing to eat until he learnt his work. Mrs Bland went back to the shop and got a bundle of food. She returned to the house with every intention of giving them the food, but George had come back and frightened her into keeping the food hidden. As he sat at the kitchen table, glowering at her, the little girl saw the bread and butter on the table, came up to him and started stroking his hand, begging for some morsel to eat. George just flicked her hand away and ignored her. Mrs Bland returned to the shop. A few minutes later she saw the wan and skeletal face

Squalid living conditions were the day to day experience for most working class people. The author

of German looking in at the window. The boy was covered in fresh bruises. Mrs Bland brought him into the shop and gave him the food.

Weeks passed and German and the other children became steadily more emaciated. Ann and George Wheatcroft would leave them locked in the house whilst they went out to the pub, sometimes from early afternoon until very late at night. When George was out at work she would suddenly lose her temper, strip German naked in the courtyard and beat him with a cane until she was exhausted. Jane Cheadle, Eliza Simpson and the other neighbours would grab the cane from her hand if they caught her, but there was little they could do when the abuse happened inside. One occasion the screams from inside were so bad that they did barge open the back door to find that Ann had stripped all three children and was once again thrashing them.

Matters were going from bad to worse. German, the oldest child, was begging for scraps of food from the other houses in the street. Everyone tried to sneak him snacks when Ann wasn't looking, but he was getting thinner and thinner. When she found out he had been begging, she tied his hands together and then tied him to the door so he couldn't get out. Ann's 'punishments' were getting increasingly barbaric. Sarah Smith saw her accuse German of begging, and when he denied it, she threw a sheet over his head and dragged him down into the cellar. She then went and borrowed a garden fork from Mr Cleaver, and went back into the cellar. Sarah stood there horrified as she heard a sickening thud and then a piercing scream from the boy. A few minutes later the boy was dragged back out the cellar, with a huge gash across his forehead.

It had gone on for long enough. Everyone in the street was revolted by this wicked woman's conduct. From Mrs Bland who tried to keep the lad alive with illicit snacks, Jane Cheadle, Eliza Simpson and Sarah Smith whose lives were constantly interrupted by the screams and beatings, to Mary Baker whose attempts to feed German through an open window were thwarted when Ann nailed it shut. Even the landlord of the local pub, Richard Hewson, had heard all the gossip almost every night. Something had to be done.

Richard Hewson just happened to be walking past Ann Wheatcroft's house on 26 March when virtually all the women from several courts in the street burst in and dragged Ann Wheatcroft out. They hauled her into the yard and held the struggling virago under the water pump. There she got a good traditional ducking, and probably a good kicking too. George was also dragged from the house. Richard took the opportunity to grab the children and take them to his pub the *Woodman* in Lower Ann Street.

The children were extremely thin and dirty. Mrs Cooke washed and tended to them in the pub, while Mr Hewson called in a doctor to see German. He still had a massive cut on his forehead, big enough to lay your little finger in according to Mrs Bland. The two younger children rallied and started to put on weight almost straight away. German was far more ill. He was now eight years old and should have weighed around 50 or 60

Did Ann Wheatcroft exert a malign influence over her husband? Strand Magazine

lbs, in fact he weighed just 23.

Over the next weeks several doctors tried to get him to rally, but he was so malnourished that the wound on his head refused to heal properly. His body was covered with other cuts and bruises as well. By 12 April he started to become delirious and despite a nutritious diet and twenty-four hour care, an infection set in to the head wound. On the 26 April his abused and battered soul took flight. Ann Wheatcroft was charged with manslaughter.

The case came to court on 7 August. Both Ann and George were charged with manslaughter. Most of the women in the street came to give evidence. This was unusual in itself, usually the inhabitants of the warrens of back to backs stayed as far from the courts and police as possible. The conclusion of the case was that George had never been seen abusing the children and thus was not guilty of the manslaughter. Ann was found guilty of cruelty and manslaughter. However, if it was proved that George was married to Ann, then he would have to take responsibility for her actions. George must have been relieved that he had never formally married her. He was humiliated in the court when the judge said that she must have gained a malign influence over him which prevented him stopping her abuse of his children.

Ann Wheatcroft was sentenced to fifteen years transportation. It was a dreadful sentence, sometimes it took over a year to reach Australia, in the most primitive conditions on a stinking old hulk. Women destined for such a fate were likely to be raped and abused on board the ship, and that was nothing to what awaited them in a penal colony. The general opinion was that she deserved every second of it.

CHAPTER 7

Mary Ball

NUNEATON

1849

*His stomach was severly swollen and the
doctor was called.*

A little girl was born to the newly married Isaac and Alice Wright in June 1818 in the parish of Nuneaton. She was christened Mary on the 28th and unlike many youngsters of that age, managed to survive her childhood. Isaac Wright was an innkeeper and so was probably wealthy enough to provide stability and food for his family, but not so wealthy that he became involved in the

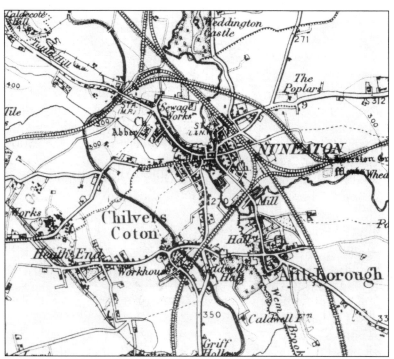

Victorian Nuneaton. Author's collection

waves of bankruptcies that swept through the county as bank after bank collapsed after the Napoleonic Wars. A couple of years later, in 1821, a lad called Thomas was born to Thomas and Hannah Ball in the town as well. The two children's destinies were going to be tragically intertwined in the succeeding years.

Time passed and nature took its course. Thomas Ball married Mary Wright in 1837 and soon enough their first child was born, only to die within its first year. Undismayed, they carried on and another child was born a couple of years later, and the tragedy was repeated. This ghastly scenario haunted them. By the start of 1847 Mary had borne five children and every one had died within twelve months. Mary was pregnant once again and the couple were living in a run down tenement in Back Lane. The constant drain on Mary's strength and disappointment for her husband of this long battle for a child had taken its emotional toll. Thomas Ball was constantly having affairs with other women, drinking heavily, and treating Mary in a most brutal manner. For Thomas, having a brood of healthy children was proof of his virility, and Mary was failing to give him that proof. Infant mortality in all towns, Nuneaton included, was stagger-ingly high in those days. The state of the town's drainage was a major cause of disease, with animal and human waste left to trickle down the roads. It polluted the wells and epidemics of cholera were a regular occurrence. Typhoid was another disease that attacked towns with equally devastating results on the children. It wouldn't be for another decade that most Midlands towns were to be able to raise the funds to build sewers.

On 20 January 1847 their sixth child was born, a little girl christened Mary Ann. Against all the odds she managed to survive her first year. Thomas now had a regular income working on the Trent Valley Railway, but the survival of the baby didn't improve his treatment of Mary. He continued to go off with other women and beat Mary when he came home drunk. It isn't much of a surprise to hear that Mary was overheard telling him: 'I wish the wagon train may pass over you.' She just got yet another beating for her pains.

Thomas' treatment of Mary was well known throughout the town. His brutal attitude led her to look for comfort and consolation elsewhere. By the middle of 1848 she started an affair with the lodger in the house next door, a lad of just nineteen called William Bacon. Nuneaton wasn't a vast anonymous city like London or Birmingham, so gossip soon got around. William was her husband's sister's brother-in-law; small towns can be a bit like that. Thomas' sister soon found out what was going on and made sure he knew all about it. Matters weren't helped by the state of the buildings in Back Lane either. Thomas Ball managed to spy on Mary and William through a crack in the wall between the houses. What he saw was enough to drive him into a violent fury.

In the first months of 1849 Thomas had to go away for a while on the railway. It gave Mary a brief respite from the beatings and abuse. It wasn't to last and he was back home by May. Absence had clearly not made their hearts grow fonder. Their rows could be heard right through the walls of the old houses. 'You are a witch!' he shouted at her. 'Well, if I am one, I'll be one,' she retorted darkly.

'Before he serves me that trick again, I'll poison him,' she told one of her friends after yet another row.

Somehow everyday life had to go on, especially with the baby growing up. Today one's thoughts might be turning towards divorce by this stage, or even just running away. In the 1840s the only way to get a divorce was by getting a private Act of Parliament, and this was not an option for anyone but the aristocracy. Running away was not possible either. Mary could have gone to the workhouse if she was destitute, but if her husband said he could keep her they would just hand her straight back to him. She was effectively a piece of his property. If she ran away to another parish and applied for workhouse relief there, they would simply cart her back to her native parish. A clue to the only way out was clear enough in the wedding vows... 'till death do us part'. It was just a matter of whose death.

One of the many little irritants of Victorian life was bed bugs. If you were rich it was easy enough to burn the old mattress and buy another. For ordinary working people this just wasn't an option. You could catch the little monsters, but they were tough nuts to kill and it was a lot easier to poison them. Some arsenic powder mixed with salt around the bedstead would see them off a treat. Of course you did need to be very careful with the arsenic.

In mid-May Mary Ball and Mrs Nicholson visited the

Arsenic was widely used in the nineteenth century to kill fleas and bed bugs as well as larger vermin. Most of the world's supply of arsenic was mined in Cornwall as a by-product of copper mining. The author

druggist 'Richardson's'. Mr Iliffe sold her a pennyworth of arsenic. He poured it out onto a sheet of paper and before he wrapped it up, warned her that it was a deadly poison. 'Such a bit as this would not poison anyone – would it?' 'Yes, half that,' he answered. Mary laughed and said: 'Good God, such a bit as that!' A plan may well have been stirring in her mind.

Once she returned to the house in Back Lane she mixed up the arsenic with salt to make the bed bug powder. However, she did not use all the mixture on the beds, she kept some wrapped in a twist of paper on the mantelpiece. She put it just beside another wrap of paper containing ordinary salt.

Thomas Ball managed to get a day off work on 18 May. He went off on a fishing trip with his friends, Joseph Petty and Thomas Watts, at nine in the morning and the three of them spent the day larking about, swimming and generally relaxing until they all returned to town at four in the afternoon. They were all starving as they hadn't taken any lunch with them, and drunk nothing but cold water.

Thomas Ball came into the kitchen and Mary gave him a bowl of gruel. He must have said he was feeling a bit tired and needed pepping up. Mary told him that there were some salts on the mantelpiece and they would do him good. She coolly watched him picked up the twist of paper. He sprinkled it over his gruel and tucked in, ravenously hungry. Perhaps she wanted to warn him that he had picked up the wrong salts, but a dozen years of infidelity, beatings and abuse soon put paid to that idea. Thomas Ball ate all the gruel, the bread ...and the arsenic. Whether by luck or judgement, the amount of arsenic left from

Mary watched implacably as her husband writhed in agony and then died.

Strand Magazine

the bed bug blitz was an exactly fatal dose.

By eight that evening Thomas Ball was in excruciating pain. His stomach was severely swollen and the doctor was called. Dr Prouse diagnosed inflammation of the bowels but there wasn't a great deal he could do about it. The family weren't rich enough to afford much in the way of medicines, and such money as they did have was needed for their one surviving child. Thomas suffered agonies through the night and the next day. He gradually weakened and at two in the morning of 20 May he finally died. Mary woke up the neighbours and called for the doctor once again. Dr Prouse looked at the corpse and issued the death certificate. Thomas Ball had died of natural causes, a stomach complaint. It wasn't an uncommon way to go in 1849.

This must have been a huge relief to Mary. From the moment Thomas had eaten the arsenic she was likely to be accused of his murder. Once he was safely buried she could start a new life, perhaps with the lad next door, William Bacon, perhaps far away from Thomas' gossiping sister. The trouble was that their rows had been heard by the whole street and most of the town had probably heard the rumour about her and William Bacon. The sudden death of Thomas gave the gossips something to really work with.

The next day, constables Vernon and Haddon turn up to ask her a few very pointed questions. Abel Vernon started with: 'Mary, your husband's gone off very suddenly; it's very alarming. I have been informed that you have been buying some arsenic.'

'Yes I have,' she answered, 'I bought it at Richardson's, used it to kill the bugs, threw the cup away and burnt the paper.'

Mary first told the officers that she had used all the arsenic to kill the bugs, but then mentioned that she had kept some back in a paper wrap on the mantelpiece. It was this inconsistency that worried the police and they decided to request a post-mortem. As the police left Mary fretted to one of her friends that had come to comfort her, that she was worried they would cut him open. 'Really?' her friend asked, for the import of what she meant was clear enough: 'I couldn't have thought that you could have done such a thing.' Mary clenched her teeth, saying: 'I've had enough to make me do that and much more.' News came back that they were indeed going to perform a post-mortem – 'If they do that, I shall be hanged.'

Mary Ball was arrested that evening. Dr Prouse and Dr George Shaw of Queens College, Birmingham quickly performed the post-mortem. Minute traces of arsenic were found in Thomas's stomach. Mary was charged with murder and conveyed to Coventry Gaol to await trial at the next assizes.

Mary was placed in the dock on 28 July. She had told a tangled and confusing tale of using the arsenic that gave the prosecution every chance of proving her guilt. She eventually settled on the story that she had left the poison on the mantelpiece and that Thomas himself had put the poison into his gruel, but by now the jury was convinced that she had deliberately set out to kill him and when they returned their verdict it was guilty, but with a recommendation to mercy. Even they had been moved by the stories of Thomas' brutality towards her and clearly thought that in some respect she had been provoked. Mr Justice Coleridge wished to know on what grounds they

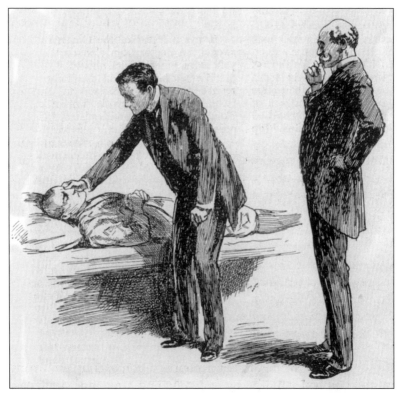

The two doctors soon discovered traces of arsenic. Strand Magazine

recommended mercy and they went into a huddle to consult each other. The trouble was there was no evidence of his brutality brought to the trial, and they then returned a verdict of guilty of murder.

Mr Justice Coleridge summed up by inferring that Thomas had become an obstacle in the way of Mary's plans and that she had shown no mercy to him, so no mercy would be extended to her. He sentenced her to death. Mary was led from the court and back to Coventry Gaol.

Once inside Coventry Gaol Mary was under pressure to make a full confession, both clear up the case and show that justice had been done, and of course to purge her soul of the sin. Mary was in no mood to do either. The prison chaplain, Reverend Chapman, decided to show her what the fires of hell were like, so that she would repent and confess. Either that or he was a sadistic bastard who liked inflicting pain on defenceless women…I'll leave that conclusion to you. He held a candle flame under her bare arm until her hand and forearm were cruelly burnt and blistered. She told him nothing, although no doubt her screams let everyone else in the prison know exactly what was going on.

The next day the prison governor, Mr Stanley, was alarmed at what was going on in his prison and called in a magistrate to investigate. Mr Bellairs got no confession out of Mary, but had sufficient evidence against Reverend Chapman to see him thrown out of the prison that very day. Not surprisingly, Mary was rather grateful to find the governor on her side even if she was due to be hung in a few days. On 5 August she finally made a confession to him detailing the exact way that the arsenic got into Thomas:

> … *I put the arsenic on the mantle-shelf, and told him there was some salts on the shelf, he might take them, they would do him good, though I knew at the time it was not salts; but I thought if he took it himself, I should not get into any scrape about it; for the people would think that he took it in by mistake.*

Mr Stanley listened to her account of him picking the wrong packet and her standing by and watching him, and was aghast at her action.

'For God's Sake, Ball, what made you do it?' he exclaimed.

'Why, my husband was in the habit of going with other women, and using me so ill; no one knows what I have suffered. But had I known as much as I do now, I would not have done it, for I would rather have left him and went to the workhouse; but I hope God will forgive me.'

Mary had only a few days left to make her peace. The vicar of St Michaels, the Reverend J B Collisson, visited her as often as he could and she became resigned to her fate. On 9 August, at ten o'clock, she was brought out of the gaol and stood on the scaffold just outside the gates. There was a crowd of around 20,000 waiting for her execution. They were quiet and respectful, quite unlike the normal rowdy mob that attended a hanging. The executioner quickly drew the bolt and Mary dropped to an instant death. The time from her ascending the scaffold to the drop was less than five minutes. For the next hour the crowd remained quiet and thoughtful, until her body was cut down and taken back into the prison for an anonymous burial.

This was to be the last public execution of a woman in Warwickshire. The little baby left orphaned by these tragic events did survive, despite such a dreadful start in life, and her descendants still live in the area today. Was Mary Ball a murderer, or someone pushed beyond the brink? It was difficult question for the judge and just as difficult a question today.

EXECUTION OF MARY BALL.
VOLUNTARY CONFESSION.

To the public, and especially to the Jurors upon whose verdict she was convicted, it will be satisfactory to know that she has left behind her a perfectly voluntary confession of her guilt; as will be found embodied in the following statement, which was handed to us yesterday morning by Mr. Stanley, Governor of the Gaol, in the presence of the Under-Sheriff, immediately after the execution:—

"For some days (says Mr. Stanley) after the trial, the prisoner appeared to be very indifferent to the awful situation to which she was placed. The Rev. H. Bellairs, Rector of Bedworth, visited her on Tuesday after the trial, and used every effort to bring her to a sense of her solemn position. He again visited her on the following Friday, and soon after his departure a change for the better was observable in the state of her feelings; and to Rebecca Vernon, a woman in waiting, she said that she had something to say, but that she would say it to the Governor, and to no one else. She also said to two other women who sat up with her the same night, 'I wish me and my husband had been separated before, and then I should not have been here.'

Warwickshire Advertiser

CHAPTER 8

Sarah Drake

NORTH LEVERTON (NOTTS)

1850

AND

Elizabeth Brandish

ETTINGTON

1897

Baby farming' was a common profession in the nineteenth century. If you happened to have an inconvenient child it was quite acceptable to pay for someone else to raise the infant. It cost money of course, but it left the mother free to pursue her career. There were a couple of cases that made the Warwickshire headlines during the course of the century. The first, that of Sarah Drake, was not directly connected with the county, but still gives a fascinating glimpse into this long forgotten practice and how the baby farmers could be utterly indifferent as to the fate of the children. The second, that of Elizabeth Brandish, shows precisely the opposite, how the surrogate parent would shift heaven and earth to ensure the child's welfare.

When Sarah Drake was about thirty-three she had a brief but very productive liaison with a Frenchman from Boulogne. The bloke promptly did a runner when he discovered she was pregnant and she was left to fend for herself. Sarah was living in her home village of North Leverton, near Nottingham, at the time, and for the first few months raised the little boy at home. It wasn't very easy for her and she decided that the best course of action was to find someone to raise the child in their family. The only other option was to have the child placed in the local workhouse. The social stigma, not to mention the utterly degrading conditions of the workhouses, were calculated to dissuade people from going there unless there was no other possible option. Even then some people preferred to die of starvation in a ditch rather than enter those dark forbidding gates.

Sarah managed to find a family in Peckham, the Johnsons, who would look after the child. In January 1848 Sarah brought the baby to them, together with some flannel for making his clothes. Mrs Johnson thought it was strange that Sarah didn't once call the baby by any name. However, a couple of weeks later she returned to see how the baby was doing and at that point she called him Lewis. It was Mrs Johnson that arranged to have the child christened and, recalling that one time she had heard the mother call him Lewis, had him christened Lewis Drake. Sarah Drake called every couple of weeks for about three months, regularly paying Mrs Johnson the six shillings a week for the child's bed and board.

After three months, Mrs Johnson received a letter from Sarah, although now she signed herself 'Taverner'. The letter may have been full of questions about 'my dear baby' but it was to mark a change in Sarah's behaviour. Apart from the occasional letter, Sarah did not once visit Mrs Johnson or her son until February 1849. The bill for the child's care gradually mounted up, so that by 1849, when Sarah reappeared, it stood at over £12, a large sum for ordinary families in those days.

Sarah now had a plan in mind. She would take the ferry over to France and place the child into the French equivalent of a workhouse, in Boulogne. She paid Mrs Johnson £1, and promised the balance when she could get it. Mrs Johnson and Sarah went to Dover station and Mrs Johnson saw Sarah go off with the child. She had insisted on keeping Lewis' clothes as a security against the outstanding debt. No doubt she had a sneaking suspicion that that would be the last she would see of Sarah Drake, little Lewis or the money.

The very next day, who should turn up on her doorstep but Sarah and Lewis Drake. The baby had become very ill on the train and a doctor had advised Sarah that Lewis had water on the brain and probably wouldn't live long. Mrs Johnson took pity on the lad and said that she would look after him for the reduced fee of five shillings a week. As she nursed the ailing child Sarah disappeared once more.

Lewis recovered quite quickly, but of his mother there was no sign apart from a growing bill for his upkeep. All through the summer Mrs Johnson fumed at the lack of funds, but she was stuck with the child and couldn't really just dump him on the street with a clear conscience. On 27 November, quite out of the blue, a letter arrived from Sarah, postmarked Edward Street, Dorset Square, London. Mrs Johnson soon made her way up there and made enquiries as to where Sarah was living. Needless to say it wasn't in Edward Street.

In fact, Mrs Johnson had missed Sarah by only a day. On 26 November she started work as a housekeeper and cook at 33 Harley Street, the household of Mr Huth. The house was a typical large London town house. On the 28th, a little after ten in the morning, Mrs Johnson finally tracked down Sarah Drake. She arrived at Harley Street and called at almost every house until she found the right one.

'Good Morning,' she said, as Sarah opened the tradesman's door.

'Good Morning Mrs Johnson, I thought I would see you about my dream.'

Slightly nonplussed, Mrs Johnson stepped into the kitchen, little Lewis Drake still holding onto her hand. Mrs Johnson told Sarah that she was very cruel to have caused her such a lot of pain and trouble. Sarah said that she couldn't help it and she couldn't send her any more money. Mrs Johnson said that it wasn't the money that had brought her there. Sarah told her that she had been going to go abroad with the family but the plan was now cancelled. Mrs Johnson didn't believe a word of this and told her so. Sarah then had to leave the parlour for a few

The upper-class houses of Harley Street were home to whole communities of servants as well as a few wealthy people. Number 33 is a specialist dental surgery today. Author's collection

minutes to attend to the mistress of the house. When she came back she took Mrs Johnson and Lewis into the housekeeper's parlour. It was a strained meeting. Mrs Johnson told Sarah that she had brought Lewis to her since there was over £9 still owing and she was not prepared to keep him any longer. Sarah begged and pleaded for her to take him back for just one more week, but Mrs Johnson was adamant. No money, no childcare.

At this point another servant, Mary Ann Wigwell, poked her nose round the door, saw that Sarah was busy and hurriedly left.

Sarah changed the subject and said how well the boy looked. Mrs Johnson told her he had got over the illness and was now a hearty little fellow. She told Sarah she had better take his hat and coat off or he would get cold, and then that he would soon need feeding.

'Very well, will he eat anything?'

'Yes,' and with that last word she turned and left the room, climbing up the iron stairs to the pavement outside. As she was nearly at the top Sarah came out and said that she would be able to get the money for the first week of January. Mrs Johnson told her sternly that her husband would be taking a summons out if she didn't pay up. Mary Wigwell watched from a corner of the kitchen, she noticed that the child was not with Mrs Johnson. She went back to the housekeeper's parlour, but the door was now locked.

Another housemaid, Sarah Powell, tried to get into the parlour, but found the door locked.

Mary Wigwell saw Sarah go back into the housekeeper's parlour and lock the door behind her. She next saw her at about twelve when the two of them were back in the kitchen preparing lunch. Mary asked what the woman had wanted with Sarah and she was told that Sarah owed her a lot of money.

Sarah said Mrs Johnson had caused her a great deal of trouble. As they were working together Sarah asked Mary if she had a box that she could have to send some old clothes to her sister in. Mary said she did have one and would let her use it. Sarah promised to get her a replacement in a few days. Mary brought the box downstairs. Mary served lunch to the family upstairs whilst Sarah went off to write a letter and pack the box.

At twenty-five to three Mary went up to the bedroom that she shared with Sarah and saw the box there, all packed up, wrapped with white cotton cloth and very securely tied with cord. There was no address card on it at that point. The box lay there for the rest of the day and next night. At seven the next morning Sarah asked Mary to carry the box downstairs. Mary was staggered to discover that the box was so heavy; she could barely lift it.

George Glass, the butler, arranged for the footman to take the box to Euston Station for Sarah. She had first asked him at three o'clock the day before, and told him it was a batch of clothes for her sister that she had meant to send before she started working at 33 Harley Street. Sarah offered William Bryant, the footman, sixpence for his trouble. William said he wouldn't take it. He told Sarah that the people at the station had said the box would be delivered to its destination that evening.

George Glass had written out the address, 'Mr Theophilus Burton, North Leverton, Nr Retford, Nottinghamshire' but it wasn't on the box itself, but on a card loosely shoved under the cords. Perhaps Sarah secretly hoped that the card would become lost, and the whole box would then go astray.

The simple but horrible truth of the matter was that as soon as Sarah had turned her back on Mrs Johnson, she saw only one way out of her trouble. There was no way that she could keep her new job with a bastard child in tow. She went back to the parlour, seized little Lewis, smashed his head against the wall, and then strangled him. She hid the body until she had the chance to pack his corpse into the box along with a few old clothes. She actually sewed the cotton up so that no one could open it up easily.

William Drake and his brother-in-law, the blacksmith Theophilus Burton, both received anonymous letters on 13 November telling them that a parcel would be arriving at the *White Hart* in Retford. William Drake went and fetched it, and took it to Theophilus's house. The loose address card finally fell off in the road a few yards from its destination. William and Theophilus cut off the cotton and forced the lock open. There was a very unpleasant sight inside: the crumpled body of a little boy. They called the local policeman.

Constable Edward Smith examined the gloomy contents of the box. On one of the aprons was a name tag – 'S. Drake'. It didn't take a great deal of speculation to work out what had happened and he reported the matter straight to the County Superintendent, Thomas Kinder.

As the grisly discovery was being made in Nottinghamshire, Mrs Johnson decided to call in on Sarah Drake. Sarah told her that she had found a friend to look after the child, and had managed to smuggle him out of the house without the masters seeing him. She also promised that she would be able to borrow the money and pay the outstanding bill. Mrs Johnson gave her the bundle of Lewis's clothes along with the bill.

'Kiss the baby for me,' she said as she left. 'Yes, I will,' replied Sarah.

Just over a week later Sarah Drake had another couple of visitors at the Harley Street house. Superintendent Thomas Kinder was accompanied by Mr Fisher of the Metropolitan Detective Police. They asked her if her name was Sarah Drake and as soon as she confirmed it, they arrested her on the suspicion of the murder of Lewis Drake. In Sarah's room were three aprons of exactly the same design as the one found inside the box. As this was taking place Mrs Johnson had been taken up to North Leverton to identify the body. She recognised the bloodstained clothes as well as the sad corpse. There was no doubt in anyone's mind what Sarah had done.

Sarah was placed in a cell under the watchful eye of Mary Ann Bridge. She was the female 'searcher' at Marylebone Station. Mary asked her what she had been charged with. Sarah asked if she was a married woman, to which she told her that she had a large family.

'You can then feel for me, and I can tell you - it's all about a child.'

Mary asked if it was a new-born.

'No, it was two years old and I hung it.' Sarah broke down and poured out the whole dreadful tale to Mary.

The case came to court in the second week of January 1850. Sarah sat in the dock, shoulders slumped forward, gazing unseeingly at the floor and sobbing gently into a white handkerchief. Despite a month in gaol she was dressed in smart respectable clothes.

Mrs Johnson broke down in tears during her evidence. She felt that she was at least partly responsible since she had simply dumped the child unannounced on Sarah. Several doctors gave evidence that Sarah must have suddenly snapped when she was first alone with the child and lashed out in blind fury. If this was the case then the jury could decide that it wasn't a case of murder, but one of manslaughter whilst temporarily insane.

After a long days trial the jury retired for fifteen minutes. When they returned their verdict was that Sarah was not guilty of wilful murder on the grounds of temporary insanity. There was a ripple of applause through the court. Sarah stood up, and then slowly collapsed in a faint.

She was confined in gaol during Her Majesty's pleasure.

Lewis Drake died directly from the violence of his mother, and indirectly because his surrogate mother washed her hands of him and sent him back because the bills went unpaid. The case of Elizabeth Brandish in 1897 was very different. For a very detailed account, have a look in my book, *Foul Deeds and Suspicious Deaths in Stratford and South Warwickshire*. Here, however, is a brief outline of the case and the role of the surrogate mother.

Elizabeth Brandish had sent her little boy to the Post family in Kent, and they had given the child to their niece, Sarah Urben, to raise. This Sarah was a very different sort of girl and quite doted on little Rees Edwards. Elizabeth Brandish had assumed the name Edwards to try to hide her identity. After a couple of years Elizabeth came down to Kent to collect the child. Sarah was probably rather sad to see the lad going away, and she was alarmed to note that whilst the woman called herself Elizabeth Edwards, the name tag inside her cloak said Elizabeth Brandish. Elizabeth collected the child and said she was taking him to her relatives in Ettington, Warwickshire. Sarah was not impressed with this idea, not least because the young boy was suffering from whooping cough and not really fit enough to travel.

In spite of Sarah's protests, Elizabeth took the child to Ashford, where she bought a tin trunk before getting on the train for London. It would be interesting to find out if there was some collective memory of the way that Sarah Drake had used a box to conceal the body of her young son. If there was it would certainly explain Sarah Urben's deep unease at the way the child went away.

Elizabeth Brandish and the young boy were found in the

street, in London. Elizabeth was violently ill, apparently having drunk some bad brandy in a rather dodgy bar. The police matron tidied the pair up and made sure they got on the next train to Towcester. There they spent the night in a hotel and on the following day boarded the train for Ettington.

The old East & West Junction Railway ran from Towcester, through Kineton and Stratford to a junction at Broom. It was a dilapidated ruin of a railway, notorious for the lateness of its ancient trains. Elizabeth and Rees boarded a Third Class carriage at Towcester, which was a large open carriage with lots of bench seats. Almost immediately, Elizabeth asked to be upgraded to Second Class and was given a compartment to herself in another carriage. This wasn't a corridor train so once the train set off the two of them were alone. The guard walked the length of the train at Kineton station and saw little Rees kneeling on the seat and looking out of the window. That was the last anyone saw of Rees Brandish.

Elizabeth got off the train at Ettington, together with the trunk, but without her son. She then spent a couple of days at her brother's farm before returning to her lodgings in Clent. The tin trunk went with her. At this point the local carter thought that it was quite heavy. It was there that she was about to become engaged to the local bobby, Sergeant Narramore. It may well have been this engagement that had spurred her into doing something about the child. Sergeant Narramore would have wanted to know why she was paying out regular sums to the Post family. After only a couple of days Elizabeth took the train back to Ettington, with the trunk. A short while later she returned to Clent once more, again with the trunk. The trunk was now suspiciously light.

Sarah Urben was beside herself with worry. She had written to Elizabeth at Ettington asking how the child was getting on, and received a reply to the effect that Rees was perfectly alright, eating well and a little wonder. Sarah knew that this couldn't possibly be right; the child had got whooping cough, was off his food and was a whining monster when he was ill. Sarah wrote to the vicar of Ettington expressing her concerns. The vicar was quite ignorant of any child at the farm and wrote back asking what she was going on about. Sarah Urben went to the police in Kent and they in turn contacted the Warwickshire

Constabulary. There was no child at the farm and so they interviewed Elizabeth Brandish in Clent.

Elizabeth told them that the previous summer she had met a woman out on the Clent Hills who had told her she was childless. As an act of charity Elizabeth said she could have her little boy. That was why she collected Rees from Kent and arranged to meet the woman on the train and hand over her child. It was a pity that she had quite forgotten to make a note of the woman's name.

If the case wasn't so important, such a tale would have had the police laughing in the aisles. They didn't believe a word of it, but Elizabeth stuck by every word and they had to prove that she was lying. After a week of searching for this strange woman they decided to arrest Elizabeth and search in real detail. The railway was searched, as was the route from the station to the farm, all with no sign of the child. Perhaps her bizarre story was true. Detective Inspector Ravenhall was determined to find the truth. Sarah Urben had now travelled up from Kent and was staying in the village anxiously awaiting news of the child she had so lovingly raised. On 13 November 1897 her worst fears were realised; the body of a young boy was discovered in a shallow grave in the vegetable garden of the farm.

Today that would have wrapped up the case pretty thoroughly, but in 1897 matters were by no means so simple. The body had been buried in quicklime and was dreadfully corroded by this ferocious chemical. It was impossible for anyone, least of all for the traumatised teenage Sarah, to identify accurately. The body had the same number of teeth as the missing child, and that was about as close as they could get to identification. It really wasn't adequate to sustain a case of wilful murder. The first trial of Elizabeth fell apart in 1898, and the jury could not agree at the end of the second. Elizabeth Brandish may well have given her bastard child to a total stranger, it could not be proved that the body that was found on the farm was that of the child. It was small consolation for the teenage Sarah Urben who had raised the little boy.

CHAPTER 9

Matilda Cooper & other Feisty Females
LEAMINGTON, WARWICK AND BIRMINGHAM
1850–1895

Mr Jeafferson was hopping mad.

Matilda Cooper was a definite rogue who could hold her own against any number of male con men. Indeed, she kept a couple of blokes handy to dispose of the goods that she managed to wheedle out of credulous souls.

Matilda must have thought she was on to a real winner when she called at the tradesmen's entrance of Samuel John Jeafferson's house in Leamington in the June 1850. The somewhat dim and possibly aptly named Sarah Strange, one of the servant girls in the house, answered the door. Matilda managed to convince her that she needed to have her planet ruled, an astrological process whereby her luck would change for the better. Sarah gave Matilda a whole shilling to do this bit of magic. To get that into perspective, Sarah was probably earning a shilling a week, plus her board and lodging. Matilda told her she would be back with the horoscope later.

A few days later Matilda Cooper returned, and having realised she had found a thoroughly credulous victim, told her that she needed eight shillings for the horoscope to work properly. Not surprisingly Sarah didn't have anything like that kind of money, but gave her all the cash she had and a couple of her dresses. Matilda went off to start the hocus pocus that would 'rule' her planet. She showed Sarah a piece of paper with lots of stars and occult symbols on it.

Matilda was soon back for more. On 16 July she persuaded Sarah to borrow some of her master's and mistress' belongings. Not to worry though, she would bring them straight back when the planet was properly ruled. Matilda must have been laughing her socks off when she left, carrying seven dresses, five petticoats, three brooches, two pocket handkerchiefs, one gold locket, a vinaigrette, a gold ring and £1 in loose change. William Hill and Thomas Hadden helped her squirrel away all this loot.

Sarah Strange duly waited for news from Matilda about how her planet was being ruled and her fortune changed, and waited, and waited some more. In fact her luck did change, but for the worse. Mr Jeafferson was hopping mad that his wife's dresses, jewellery and even underwear had gone missing. Some of his own shirts were missing too. Sarah had a lot of explaining to do, first to Mr Jeafferson and then to Mr Baron Platt, the judge at the Warwick Summer Assizes. Matilda and her cronies had been arrested soon after the theft was discovered. They were each sentenced to two years imprisonment with hard labour.

The rather dim Sarah Strange was not charged with theft as she acted as the principal witness at the trial, so may be her luck had changed a bit for the better; she could have gone to gaol for theft herself.

> One week Gaol.
> THE FORTUNE-TELLING CASE AT LEAMINGTON.—*Matilda Cooper*, *William Hill*, and *Thomas Madden*, were indicted for having stolen, on the 16th of July last, one gold locket, one vinaigrette, a gold ring, and numerous other articles, the goods of Samuel John Jeaffreson. The prisoners were also charged with receiving the same knowing them to have been

Author's collection

Elizabeth Davies was another character that tried to get something for nothing. On 26 September 1874 she reported her daughter-in-law, Eliza Webb, had assaulted her with a cobbler's last. She said that Eliza, her son, and another man, forced their way into her house in John Street, Warwick, and started taking out her furniture. Elizabeth tried to interfere and was knocked down in a scuffle, Eliza wielding the cobbler's last like a club.

The defence of Eliza was that nothing of the sort had happened. The judge had to listen to a complicated tale of how Elizabeth Davies had made her husband's life such a misery by beating him up, that the poor old chap was eighty, that he had moved into his daughter's house for refuge… and anyway, the drunken old boot had hated her ever since she married her father… and they had only been trying to get some of his furniture but she had sold it all and spent it on drink... and the old woman was so plastered she couldn't stand up and fell, banging her head on the floor... twice... and another thing...

Oh dear.

The judge simply threw the whole case out of court and demanded every one pay their costs.

The Warwick judges had to have the patience of a saint and the wisdom of Solomon.

Another classic scrap took place in the Commercial Buildings in Saltisford, Warwick, between some of the dressmakers who lived there. They were a ferocious lot, and when some of the Atkins girls also started dressmaking, relations

Sometimes the lawyers had their work cut out. Strand Magazine

between them and the Barnacle family soured. On 20 June 1888 the simmering feud finally blew up.

Alice Barnacle went out for a walk at nine that night. She was a fairly old lady and lived with her son, William, and his wife, Annie. As she passed her neighbour's house Lucy Atkins started yelling insults at her. She walked on, probably muttering about the youth of today. However, on her return half an hour later Lucy was still there and a regular shouting match began. Annie Barnacle came out to back up her mother-in-law. Lucy Atkins then called her sister, Emily, out of their house. Emily came out holding her baby. She promptly hit Annie Barnacle who responded by thumping her right back, and kicking and biting her. Emily screamed for her other sister, Mary Ann Atkins. Mary Ann took the baby off Emily, but Alice Barnacle was now trying to thump her. William Barnacle came out and grabbed Emily by the hair as Annie was trying to hit her. Things were getting somewhat confused by now and no one could accurately say who was hitting who. Fists, teeth and boots were flying all over the place. Alice Barnacle managed to get in a massive blow to Mary Ann Atkin's head, and cut it wide open. She was wearing a very solid wedding ring, nearly as good as a knuckle-duster. The blood flew everywhere and William Barnacle decided enough was enough; he dragged his mother back into the house. Mary Ann had her wound dressed by William Luggett, a labourer who also lived in Commercial Buildings, and was a very sorry sight by the time the police arrived. Lucy Atkins did a runner and by the time the case came to court the following week, had moved to Rowington.

The magistrates listened with a sense of growing confusion to the various plaintiffs and defendants. Finally, they called Mrs Davies, an older lady who lived there, for an account of what she saw. Her comment was that ever since she had lived there she thought that they were a quarrelsome lot. This was pretty much what the magistrates had concluded and they dismissed the case telling each party to pay their own costs or face prison.

Lizzie Brown was another harridan. She was charged along with her husband with maliciously wounding Gervais Simonon with intent to do him some grievous bodily harm. Gervais was their lodger in 1874 and had never been any trouble at all. He had a room in their house in Whittall Street, Birmingham. However on 20 November he came home in the evening and said that he would be leaving at the end of the week. William Brown suddenly took against him and said that if he was going to leave then he had better leave straight away. Gervais said that

---

CRUEL OUTRAGE AT BIRMINGHAM.—*William Brown*, 26, porter, and *Lizzie Brown*, his wife, were indicted for having, at Birmingham, on the 20th of November last, maliciously wounding Gervais Simonon, with intent to do him some grievous bodily harm.—Mr. Buzsard was for the prosecution, and Mr. Harris for the prisoners.—In November the prosecutor lodged at the house of the prisoner in a court leading out of Whittall-street, Birmingham. One evening he went home, and said that he would leave his lodgings on the following day. The male prisoner told him he had better go at once if he intended to leave. Thereupon the prosecutor said he had paid for the lodgings until the Saturday, and would not go until that day. The male prisoner seized him by a certain part of the body, and caused the most excruciating agony. A

Warwickshire Advertiser

he had paid for his lodgings until Saturday and would leave when he was good and ready. William went berserk and a scuffle started. Lizzie wasn't going to be left out of this fight and wrestled Gervais to the ground, holding him there whilst her husband gave him kick after kick into his groin. Gervais was screaming in agony and yelling: 'Let me go, let me go.'

Outside, a certain Mrs Walton heard the screams and called for the police to come. She then booted the front door open and was stunned to see Gervais stagger out, William Brown hanging onto his waist and Lizzie Brown hanging off his neck. Lizzie pinioned Gervais against the wall and her husband started kicking him in the groin again. Mrs Walton was having none of this and waded into the fight herself, knocking both William and Lizzie off the young man who collapsed exhausted to the ground. He was brutally bruised and covered in bite marks. William was sentenced to fifteen years and Lizzie to five. The indomitable Mrs Walton was given a reward of £3 by the judge.

Families could cause no end of trouble. The Parker family lived in one of the courts off Dollman Street in Birmingham in 1895. There was just Mr and Mrs Parker and their daughter, Clara, but they could terrify an entire neighbourhood. Another family living in the same court was the Banners. Elizabeth and Henry Banner had just the one son, Henry. On 23 April Elizabeth Banner went out into the courtyard to hang up some of her washing to dry. Jane Parker was feeling in a particularly malicious mood, so she took out her hearth rug and proceeded to beat the dust out of it right underneath Mrs Banner's clean clothes. She was utterly furious and swore that she would tell Mr Frederick Parker just how spiteful and vindictive she had been.

After fuming all afternoon, Mrs Banner saw Frederick Parker get home from work, and so she went and banged on their door. Just as she was about to tell Frederick the story about the washing, Jane Parker bustled up and shouted: 'You b____, you are trying to set him on me. I will smash your face in.'

Jane Parker started to thump Elizabeth Banner with her fists. Almost as soon as the scuffle started Clara Parker came out of the house and joined in. Clara grabbed Mrs Banner's hair and held her down so that Jane could repeatedly bash her in the face and about the head. At one point Mr Parker took a swing at her too, although after that he tried to calm his wife and daughter down and get them off her. It wasn't until one of the neighbours, Mrs White, stormed out of her house and separated them that Elizabeth Banner could break free. She limped back to her house bleeding from several head wounds as well as a black eye and bloody nose.

Henry Banner got home from work to find his son, Arthur, trying to dress her wounds. Elizabeth was not in the best of health before the fight and in the days afterwards she started to become increasingly dazed and confused. By the end of April she was completely losing her sanity and on 1 May she was taken into the city asylum in a manic state. Within a few days she started to lapse into a coma and on 6 May she died. The post-mortem showed that she had suddenly developed meningitis. Mr and Mrs Parker and their daughter were arrested, and at the coroner's inquest, even though the doctors would not commit themselves as to the cause of the illness, they were sent for trial on a charge of manslaughter. After a few months in prison it seems that they were acquitted because the doctors would not commit themselves as to whether the beating she had taken contributed to the onset of her illness.

Birmingham can be a tricky place to live!

Frederick Drew was quite the ladies man. In fact he managed to sweet talk Lizzie Hawkes away from her husband and into bed with him. Lizzie was just a young woman, well dressed and very attractive. She lived in Vaughan Street, Birmingham and worked nearby as a tailoress. Her husband was not in the least impressed by her gallivanting off with Frederick, but he was completely besotted with her and spent the next few months listlessly waiting for her to come back.

Five months passed by with Frederick and Lizzie enjoying their affair. Lizzie introduced him to her family, which was a mistake considering she had an even more attractive younger sister. Frederick then managed to work his way through her savings and started to beat her up when she complained. Things were not looking bright for Lizzie. The fizz rapidly faded and Frederick started seeing Lizzie's sister more frequently. Eventually Lizzie's money ran out, and so did Frederick – the bounder.

Frederick Drew moved in with Lizzie's sister at the start of July. As far as Lizzie was concerned this was a declaration of war. She went completely wild, swearing she would tear him apart. On the afternoon of the 6th, she hid a large carving knife under her apron and laid in wait for him. Frederick had to go down an alleyway to get to her sister's front door and Lizzie lurked in a dark corner waiting for him to come back from work.

Frederick Drew was no doubt feeling pretty chuffed with himself as he turned into the alley, expecting to enjoy an intimate evening with Lizzie's sister. He wasn't expecting to find Lizzie leaping out of a doorway at him wielding a foot long knife. He turned and ran as fast as he could towards the door. Lizzie managed to get one hefty slash of the knife into his back and he was out of reach. She sprinted down the alley after him and managed to slice his cheek open with another wild blow. Frederick put on an extra burst of speed, hurtled through the door and slammed it behind him. The knife was wedged between the door and post, the blade twanging with malice.

If Frederick thought he had got away with it, he didn't realise just how furious Lizzie was. She started to batter against the door with her whole weight. The hinges bent and the panels cracked. Frederick backed away in horror as he realised that Lizzie was going to stop at nothing short of his complete annihilation. The door wasn't going to stop her for long. The courtyard outside rang to her screams and threats and the door started to give way. Frederick cringed up against the fireplace, and then realised that his only hope was to use the poker to fight back. He picked it up just as the door shattered and Lizzie erupted inside swinging the carving knife with mortal intent. He quickly bashed her over the head with the poker and she went down like a sack of potatoes.

By now half the courtyard was full of people and someone had sent for the police. Frederick Drew heaved a huge sigh of relief. Lizzie however leapt up again and tried to go for his throat. He managed to swipe the knife out of her hand with the poker, shattering it into a dozen pieces. Still screaming insults and abuse at him, she was overpowered by the crowd and pinned down until the police arrived. She still hadn't calmed down as they dragged her off to the Queens Hospital. The last Frederick heard was her shrieking that she would get him again, and this time put some powder behind it (a reference to using a gun).

'Revenge is sweet,' she yelled at him and she would have it.

A very chastened Frederick Drew prosecuted Elizabeth Hawkes for stabbing him. The judge listened with growing incredulity to the story of how he had dumped her for her sister, spent all her money and beaten her up. He was not in the least impressed with his behaviour and called Lizzie's first husband into the court. Would he take her back and keep her under control? He was clearly delighted and said he would. The judge ordered him to do so, and then, although Lizzie was clearly guilty of the offence, deferred the sentence to another time. I could find no reference to the sentence ever being imposed.

CHAPTER 10

Sarah Pinkard
THRUPP
1851

Sarah was a particularly nasty piece of work. By 1851 she lived just outside Warwickshire in a place called Thrupp towards Daventry. She was now on her third husband, John Pinkard, and realised there may be a way of getting her hands on his family money.

John Pinkard was the son of Richard and Elizabeth, an elderly couple now, who lived a short distance away from John's farm on the Long Buckby Road. Elizabeth had an uncle who had died the year before and left a trust of a thousand pounds. The interest from this was to be paid to Elizabeth until she died, and then the whole sum was to be divided up between her children. John was her only child, and so on her death he would become staggeringly wealthy. Sarah, who had been brought up in a poor family and started her working life as a domestic servant, was more than a little tempted by this vast fortune. The only problem was that, although Elizabeth was heading towards sixty years old, she was in fine health. Sarah didn't think that this was really fair and wondered how matters could be hurried up. Her own circumstances were not brilliant, John's farm was not making the kind of profits it needed and debts were starting to pile up in every direction.

Sarah made a detailed and devious plan to get rid of her mother-in-law and get her hands on the money. What she needed to do was make it look as though the old lady had committed suicide. Towards the end of September, Elizabeth herself gave her one idea; Elizabeth needed some cloth tape to mend some shirt collars. Sarah had some in her cupboard at home, it was easily strong enough to strangle someone. With the weapon chosen, Sarah just needed an opportunity and one presented itself on the last Friday of the month.

Richard Pinkard left his cottage early in the morning. It was the day of the fair at Daventry and farmers from miles around took the opportunity to go into town, look for new farm hands and sell their crops. The farmers, and indeed the whole population, intended to have a good time in the stalls and pubs of the town. John Pinkard also went to the fair, leaving Sarah at home with the servants and farm labourers. Around nine o'clock Sarah told the domestic servant, Ann Frost, to go to Wilton and buy some bread since they were running low. With one less witness about, Sarah put on her bonnet and shawl and set off across the greensward towards Thrupp. As the clock was striking ten Thomas Hadland, one of the farm labourers saw her walking straight towards the old Pinkard's house.

Even though half the population had gone to the fair in Daventry, there were still plenty of people about. John Letts and John Lyddington were working on the road not far from the old Pinkard's cottage. Both of them saw a woman appear from the footpath from John Pinkard's farm at Thrupp Ground, and go into the cottage. They were about a hundred yards away and so did not recognise who this woman was. They could just hear the sound of voices coming from inside.

The road was fairly busy. At eleven twenty-five William Reynolds, the constable from Long Buckby, was walking past. He noticed the front door open and standing just inside was Sarah. He didn't speak to her, but he made a note of seeing her then in his notebook when he wrote it up later that day. He was quite certain that it was her because he had seen her many times before. Another man was passing at about the same time. William Cole noticed a woman rummaging about in the flower pots on the window sill, and then step out of the front door, look both ways along the road and disappear back indoors.

A few minutes later she was back out again. Frank Darlow was riding past on his horse. He knew

She went back into the cottage with murder in mind. Strand Magazine

Sarah and she asked him if he was riding to the fair. He told her he had to go to Norton to get his horse shod. She went back into the cottage.

As Frank rode off Martha Marks, Emma Marks and Caroline Tredgold were leaning on a gate a little way off down the road having a good gossip. Suddenly they thought that they heard a cry of 'Murder!' several times. The three women weren't sure if they had heard right and waited to see if the cry was repeated. It wasn't. Thomas Flowers walked past the cottage, and heard a groaning sound as though someone was very ill inside. He slackened his pace to see if it was something he should be attending to. The noise ceased as he passed the door, but started again as he went carried on.

If any of the three women or Thomas had stepped through the door of the cottage they could have saved the old lady. As it was they were the unwitting witnesses of a foul murder. Inside the dark cottage, Sarah Pinkard smashed her mother-in-law's head against a wall, swinging her across the room by her arm. Elizabeth tried to save herself by grabbing Sarah's dress, ripping some of the cloth out of the gather at the waist band. The old woman simply did not have the strength to put up a fight against the well built younger woman. Groaning, Elizabeth fell to the floor and Sarah seems to have picked up a mallet and bashed her again. As Elizabeth lay on the floor Sarah hit her once again, this time with a cosh. The blow to her skull just above her right eye knocked her unconscious. It was a small mercy in view of what Sarah had in mind for her next. Sarah reached into her pocket and pulled out a roll of linen ribbon, the very stuff that Elizabeth had wanted to repair those collars. She wrapped one end around the old ladies throat and tightened it until Elizabeth Pinkard was completely strangled.

Sarah's violence was quite premeditated. She now propped up the body on a chair and tied the other end of the tape to the ceiling joist. To all appearances Elizabeth Pinkard had now committed suicide. Although she was sitting on a chair, the weight of her torso pulled the tape tight, partially supported. As her body swung slowly from side to side, Sarah slipped out of the door and hurried back to her farm.

John Letts and John Lyddington watched her go.

Satisfied that she had committed the perfect murder, Sarah

hurried back to the farm. When she got back, Ann Frost had returned from her errands. Ann pointed out that Sarah's dress was torn about the waist and stained with something red. Thomas Hadland had noticed as well. Sarah told both of them that she had been picking blackberries and it had got stained and torn in the brambles. She changed the dress and washed it straight away.

The dreadful news of Elizabeth Pinkard's suicide broke when Mr Bird called at the cottage mid-afternoon. He pushed open the door to see Elizabeth half sitting on the chair, her torso and head swinging from the linen tape. Letts and Lyddington came running at his shouts, and within the hour they had called in Dr Sharman. John Letts ran down to Thrupp Ground farm and told Sarah. She seemed a bit put out and asked him to go with her to the cottage. At the cottage John Pinkard arrived and escorted Sarah home without saying a word. Dr Sharman began his examination, and he was deeply worried by the strange posture of the old lady. He didn't think that she could have hung herself in that position, and why was there blood on the wall well away from where the body was? Richard Pinkard arrived back from the fair having heard the dreadful news. He confirmed to the doctor that there had been no blood on the wall when he had left that morning. He also told the doctor that there had been no linen tape in the house either.

That dark Friday night Ann Frost kept vigil with Richard over Elizabeth's body. The following day Doctor Sharman made a far more detailed examination of the body. Elizabeth had two massive bruises on her skull, one on the top and one over the eye. No matter how she had struggled she could not have received both those injuries accidentally. He was convinced that this was a murder, not a suicide. He requested the local coroner for a post-mortem and inquest.

Dr Sharman decided to see what Sarah had to say about the matter. She matched the description of the road workers and she may well have had a motive. On Sunday morning he spoke to her at the farm. He asked her if she had heard any of the rumours about Elizabeth's death. She said she had not. He then told her that he was certain that it was a case of murder not suicide. She agreed with this and told him: 'Be it who it may, I hope they will be discovered and punished.'

The doctor asked if she knew whom it might be, but she told him that she had no idea. She had talked it over with her husband and they couldn't think of anyone who would want to do anything like this. She went on to describe her mother-in-law as: 'She was a quiet and peaceable woman, one that you might live and die with and not have a word amiss.'

She told the doctor that she had not seen Elizabeth since the previous Sunday evening. All her protestations of innocence did little to calm the doctor's suspicions and he took the appropriate steps.

Constable Edmund Osborne arrived at Thrupp Grounds. He found Sarah some fifty yards down the road and escorted her back to the house. There he searched her room and chest of drawers. He found a roll of linen tape of exactly the same type as that which strangled Elizabeth. He also found a couple of coshes, one of which had bloodstains on it. He then found an apron and shawl, both of which had blood stains on them too. The shawl had been hidden behind some furniture. He told Sarah: 'No doubt some person has committed this deed that has some interest in it.'

She replied: 'I am sure I don't wish to take Mrs Pinkard's life, or any other person's, for the sake of money; for I have plenty of money in my own house and can have plenty more for sending for.'

It wasn't quite the answer that the constable was expecting considering that a law suit was now being taken out for the repayments of John Pinkard's debts. He promptly arrested her.

That evening, John Pinkard went to Thomas Hadland's cottage in Daventry. He offered him some tobacco and had brought a bottle of ale for him.

'I want you to go to Thrupp to sleep tonight. It's a serious job, they have fetched my wife on suspicion of that case, and you can prove that she did not leave the whole of the day.'

Thomas looked him the eye and said: 'No, I cannot, for she was out.'

John persuaded him out into the street, saying: 'Jump up behind me, my nag will carry double'

Thomas said he would rather walk across the fields, and once John was out of sight, turned back home, he had had enough of the pair of them. He stayed in Daventry, quite certain that he

Ashow churchyard, the scene of the exhumation. The author

summer to work in the Shakespeare household. In addition to the butchery shop Mrs Shakespeare took in lodgers and through the summer of 1851 Mr and Mrs Norrington were staying at the house. The Shakespeares had no children, so there was plenty of room. Sarah had to do virtually all the household tasks, from washing and cooking to changing the beds and setting the tables. She was given a room upstairs, and even a mattress to sleep on. There was just one sheet and a thin blanket. Of course she had to be fed, but her dinner consisted

KENILWORTH.

ALLEGED DEATH FROM THE ILL-TREAT-MENT OF A SERVANT GIRL—EXHUMATION OF THE BODY, AND CORONER'S INQUISITION.

A servant girl of the name of Sarah Morris, having died very recently at her mother's house in Ashow, and in consequence of reports having been circulated that her death had been caused by the ill-treatment of her master and mistress, the former named Shakespeare, a butcher, at Leamington, W.

Warwickshire Advertiser

of the fat from the mutton, not the meat. As the weeks passed she found herself going to bed exhausted, cold and hungry. Her wages amounted to a shilling a week.

After eight weeks Sarah found that her stomach was getting increasingly upset and visited the chemists in Kenilworth. She bought some tincture of rhubarb, the usual remedy for a runny tummy. For a mild disorder it was adequate, but Sarah was getting very ill indeed, and starting to become too weak to do her job properly. Mrs Shakespeare was in the position to know that Sarah was increasingly sick, but took no notice at all. As the days passed Sarah weakened noticeably, but she received neither care nor respite from her heavy workload. On Friday 26 September she was barely able to stand but Mrs Shakespeare still insisted that she pump the water, wash out the shop and tend to the lodgers. Her evening meal probably made things worse, some beef that had seen better days with a serving of kidney beans.

Ashow was a small agricultural village in 1851. The author

By Saturday 27 September, Sarah was extremely ill. She was suffering from dysentery and stomach cramps. She begged to go home to her mother, but Mrs Shakespeare was having none of that and insisted that she carried on with her duties. When Mr Shakespeare came home in the evening he noticed she was looking ill and insisted that she took some powder of rhubarb. Rhubarb has the effect of purging the bowels, perfect if you are constipated, but if you already have dysentery it is probably one of the worst medicines you could try. By the end of the day she was in a dreadful state. All she had to eat or drink was a couple of cups of cold coffee.

Sunday found Sarah even worse, unable to work and barely able to control her bowels. Sarah struggled to make it to the privy but failed. Mrs Shakespeare went wild, screaming: 'Dirty wretch!' repeatedly; then forced Sarah to fetch a pail of water from the pump and wash down her bedroom floor. That evening she was too weak to even lay the table. Mrs Shakespeare scolded her and once again called her a wretch. Mr Shakespeare suggested she had a glass of brandy with cayenne pepper. Sarah lay there suffering from cramps and begged to go home again. Mrs Shakespeare still refused, and wouldn't even let Sarah write a letter to her mother. That night Sarah slept on her damp, cold mattress with a thin sheet over her, shivering from illness as much as the September night air. She moaned and groaned during the night. On Monday morning she couldn't get out of bed. Mrs Shakespeare was not impressed.

At this juncture, if not long before, most people would have sent for a doctor. It would be expensive, medical care cost money in Victorian times, but it was the responsibility of the Shakespeares to look after their servants. Mrs Shakespeare did nothing of the sort, she finally told Sarah that she could go home if she wasn't able to work. Sarah just lay on her bed. She was pretty much past caring. Mrs Shakespeare told her husband to get rid of her.

In 1851 local transport was all by horse, cart, or walking. The carts ran between the towns and villages on turnpike roads, which had tollgates every few miles where you had to pay a toll. To get Sarah home Mr Shakespeare told his younger brother Joseph to make ready their cart and pony. Mrs Shakespeare told Sarah to get her belongings together, they amounted to a bundle of clothes weighing in excess of twenty pounds. Sarah waited in the kitchen, weak but eager to be out of this callous household. Once Joseph had got the cart ready Mr Shakespeare gave him three pence to pay for the toll and went to tell Sarah the cart was ready. She clambered aboard and sat on the bench seat beside Joseph.

Mr Shakespeare now changed his mind and told Joseph to set her down by the stile leading to the village of Ashow, and told Sarah that she would have to walk the rest of the way. Joseph gave him the three pence back since he would now drive along Sandy Lane rather than the turnpike road. Sandy Lane was then a potholed, deeply rutted farm track rather than the well surfaced gravel turnpike. They set off around lunchtime.

The constant bouncing and jolting soon had Sarah moaning in pain again and she curled up in a ball of pain on her bundle of clothes in the back of the cart. In a couple of hours they reached the stile and Joseph helped her down and onto the footpath. He asked if she was feeling strong enough to walk the rest of the way, and in her eagerness to get home she rather foolishly said that she was. Joseph left her and returned to Kenilworth. Sarah picked up the heavy bundle of clothes, basket and umbrella, and set off across the fields. Over the entire weekend she had had just three cups of cold coffee, a sip of brandy and some rhubarb powder. She was now in the throes of serious dysentery. The sun was setting and the dew of an autumn night started to fall.

Elizabeth Haycock and her father were walking along the footpath later that evening when they discovered Sarah collapsed on the ground, barely alive. She was covered in mud and soaking wet from repeatedly falling over as she struggled with her fading strength to get home. They managed to lift her up and carry her back to her mother's house in the village. At half past eight Sarah's mother, Mrs Bryan, tried to revive her by putting her freezing feet in a bowl of warm water, then wrapped her up in blankets and put her to bed.

For the next week Sarah hovered on the edge of death. The exposure of the freezing night had been the final straw. Mr Ayton, the surgeon in Kenilworth, tried to rouse her and her mother constantly nursed her. Sarah was as broken emotionally as she was physically: 'Oh mother,' she sobbed, 'I don't think I shall ever get well.'

The local vicar, Reverend W Howard, came round almost every day. He comforted her with the prospect of everlasting peace in heaven, but he was wracked with guilt himself. He had directed Joseph in the cart towards the stile and failed to realise the dreadful condition Sarah was in as she lay in the back of the cart. Joseph had asked for directions on the road, and told him that he had been ordered to take Sarah to the stile, and not to go by the turnpike.

Sarah finally died on the following Tuesday and was buried in the ancient churchyard of Ashow. The rumours of poisoning and worse started almost immediately and thus it was that Mr S Poole, the district coroner, ordered her exhumation a week later. Although the jury was at pains to point out that the Shakespeares had behaved according to the prevailing standards of the day, there was still intense criticism of the system that allowed servants to be thrown out on the street if they became ill.

There seems to be no headstone for poor Sarah. It was probably only wood and has long since vanished. The author

CHAPTER 12

Ann Osborn

WARWICK

1863

Pepper Street was a hive of gossip . . .

There are some cases that baffled the legal process of the nineteenth century. In our modern high technology world there is DNA testing, CCTV and lie detectors. Back in 1863 there was only rumour, gossip and a strong belief that no one would lie after they had sworn to tell the truth on the bible. It made things a lot more vague and open to interpretation. The coroner really had his work cut out.

On 7 May 1863 the brook running to the west of Warwick town centre was swollen with flood water. It ran down the back of Pepper Street and then through the tanyard of Mr Burberry's leather works. Amongst the flotsam that washed up in the yard was the body of a child. The local surgeon was called. He concluded that baby boy was about ten days old before death. The umbilicus had healed over and the baby had been making good growth. Unfortunately, he concluded that the body had been in the water for up to a week before it had been found, and was in too poor condition for him to be able to determine the cause of death, or make any kind of identification. The inquest had to be postponed pending further information.

Further information was not long in coming forward. Pepper Street was a hive of gossip and pretty much everyone knew everyone else's business. If nothing else they were virtually all related to each other in a complex web of in-laws, siblings and mutual hatreds. A very nasty rumour soon came to the ears of the coroner. Ann Osborn had been expecting a child in April and there was no sign of the infant.

Pretty much everyone seemed to know about it except Ann. Ann Osborn was a widow with five children living in Pepper Street. Mrs Evans, the midwife who had delivered all her

The old tanning yard where the horrible discovery was made. The author

children, spoke to her in February, expecting her to say when she was due, but Ann told her that she wasn't pregnant. Somewhat surprised, Mrs Evans kept her council. Mr Stephens, the relieving officer at the workhouse, also noticed she was putting on weight in a very distinctive way. He asked her if she would be coming to the workhouse to be delivered, but again she told him that she wasn't expecting a baby. The trouble was that she hadn't remarried and Victorian social values really frowned upon illegitimate children.

For the young widow, living in poverty, there was no effective means of contraception, and her five existing children took all her money and more. She had a boyfriend, Charles Chambers, who helped her out when he could. He worked as a boatman on the Grand Junction Canal and was often away on long boat trips carrying coal and goods all around the country. Charles had been seeing her for several years, even though he was married to Ellen. This rather haphazard relationship and the insecurity

of poverty meant that an extra mouth to feed would be catastrophic for Ann. Indeed there was already a rumour going the
rounds that Ann had smothered another illegitimate child back
in 1861. Pepper Street was rife was some pretty vicious stories
about Ann.

The chief instigator of the rumours seems to have been none
other than Charles Chambers' sister, Martha Masters. She lived
a few doors down the road and seems to have taken a pretty dim
view of her brother's liaison with Ann; far worse than Charles'
wife Ellen, who seems to have taken matters in her stride.

Mrs Evans and Mr Stephens kept a watchful eye on the
gradually expanding figure of Ann Osborn. Ann was a pauper,
and with all those children she could not even afford a pair of
shoes, so she went to the workhouse and asked Mr Stephens if
he could give her a pair from the parish relief fund. He again
accused her of being pregnant and told her that he would not
give her any shoes until she admitted the fact. Ann refused and
left the workhouse doors barefoot.

March gave way to April and Ann was taken very ill one
Saturday night. Her daughter took her up a cup of tea, but
otherwise stayed downstairs looking after the other children.
The next day she was still unwell and Ellen Chambers, Martha
Masters and Mrs Benton (Ann's sister) all came round to help.

Men working on the boats could be away for weeks on end. Author's collection

Martha accused Ann of hiding the birth of a baby. Ann told her that nothing of the sort had happened. Life in the overcrowded Osborn household settled down as Ann recovered. Charles Chambers had to go on a long boat trip and was away for the next couple of weeks. When he returned the coroner was trying to identify the body found in the stream.

The inquest was resumed on 16 June. As far as Mrs Evans and Mr Stephens were concerned, Ann Osborn had given birth to a child, and then thrown it into the privy at the back of her house. This privy emptied directly into the brook that ran down to the tanyard. The coroner seems to have been fairly convinced that this was the case and intended to get the evidence to prove this. With the exception of Martha Masters the rest of the inhabitants of Pepper Street closed ranks and shut up about the whole affair. They all denied any knowledge of Ann's pregnancy.

The Wheatsheaf. *Coroner's inquests were often held in public houses since they were some of the few places that could hold enough witnesses close to the scene.*

The author

During the inquest Charles Chambers refused to admit that he had any relationship and denied offering to give her ten shillings to help her out, which his sister had told the inquest jury about. The coroner insisted that he admit that he may be the father and he consistently refused. Charles Chambers was sent to the lock-up to 'improve' his cooperation. Mrs Benton also refused to implicate her sister and was also threatened with being sent to gaol. Even Ellen Chambers, who could have been particularly jealous of Ann, also gave evasive answers. The coroner was furious, but there was very little evidence on which he could charge her. He even insisted that Ann's eleven-year-old daughter gave evidence, on the grounds that children would not lie. Presumably he had none himself. The young girl told the court of her mother's illness, but said nothing of any baby being born. This was no obstacle however, and the coroner had Ann arrested and charged with wilful murder. He had entirely forgotten that there was no formal identification of the body.

Ann languished in gaol until the August Assizes. The children had been taken to the workhouse and Pepper Street was on the brink of riot. When the case was brought before the assizes it was instantly thrown out. There was no evidence that the child found in the brook was anything to do with Ann. All the gossip and rumour that the coroner had paid such careful attention to was insufficient to mount any kind of prosecution. Quite what the truth behind it all was will never be known. If the child had been born in the cramped confines of an overcrowded house, and then been fed and tended for ten days, surely everyone in the street would have heard its cries. Babies are noisy things even when they're little angels. Perhaps in these days of DNA testing the problem could have been solved one way or another, but in 1863 it was a very different world.

CHAPTER 13

Eliza Walters and Other Ferocious Women

BIRMINGHAM, LEAMINGTON AND EDGBASTON

1830–74

She followed him down the passageway,
bawling all sorts of abuse.

Eliza Walters didn't plan to kill her husband, it just sort of happened. She had always had something of a temper and Henry tended to avoid a scene by making a speedy departure to the pub. Eliza herself wasn't averse to the odd tipple and it was to prove a lethal combination.

On the evening of the 26 June 1874, Henry had stopped off for a drink after work. He dropped in at his local, the *Shepherd's Rest*, in Bradford Street, Birmingham. He was chatting away with his friend, John Davis, another labourer, for a couple of hours. Unknown to him Eliza had been out on the booze earlier that day, but had returned home for a snooze.

Eliza woke up around nine, in a filthy mood. Henry hadn't come home yet and she was fairly sure he was spending his wages down at the pub. She pulled on her shawl and stamped off to Bradford Street to find him, stormed into the *Shepherd's Rest*, marched straight across the tap room and belted Henry in the face with her fist.

Henry was somewhat surprised by this turn of events. Eliza was shouting at him:

'You old ———, I'll kill you.'

Edward Newey, a painter who had also popped in for a quiet drink, was startled to see this drunken virago laying into old Henry. Henry lurched to his feet, he wasn't entirely sober himself, but refrained from hitting her back. He went towards the front door, presumably to either go home, or at least put some distance between himself and the furious Eliza. She followed him down the passageway, bawling all sorts of abuse. About three feet from the door she grabbed his shoulders and gave him a violent shove towards the door.

The shove propelled Henry forward, through the open door and, in a tripping, stumbling windmill of legs and arms, down the steps into the street. Henry landed head first on the pavement. He didn't move, he was completely unconscious and inert.

Eliza fretted as some people from the pub carried him back home and put him to bed. Later that night Mr William Thomas, the local surgeon, came to see Henry but there was little he could do. The Walters' household could not afford much in the way of health care and a suddenly sobered Eliza washed and watched Henry as he lay in a coma through Saturday and Sunday. Mr Thomas called round regularly, but on the Monday Henry died. His body was taken to Mr Thomas' surgery for a post-mortem.

Henry had suffered a fractured skull with massive internal bleeding when his head hit the stone pavement. Eliza was promptly charged with having feloniously killed and slain her

SLAYING A HUSBAND.—*Eliza Walters*, a middle-aged woman, was indicted for having feloniously killed and slain her husband, Henry Walters, at Birmingham, on the 29th of June.—Mr. Nathan prosecuted; prisoner was not professionally defended.—On the evening of the 26th of June the deceased had been drinking at the Shepherd's Rest public-house, Bradford-street, Birmingham.—John Davis, labourer, of 7 court, 11 house, Moseley-road, said that he joined him shortly after eight o'clock. At half-past nine the prisoner came into the bar, and struck her husband in the face. The deceased, who was tipsy, did not return the blow, but got up and went towards the front door.—Edward Newey, painter, said he heard the prisoner using abusive language towards the deceased in the passage. He saw her punch him with her fist in the corner of the taproom near the door. She was not sober. He heard her say, "You old ——, I'll kill you." As he turned to avoid her, she caught him by the shoulders and pushed him violently towards the entrance. At this time he was about a yard from some steps leading down to the street.

husband. The case came to court in the second week of July.

Eliza could not afford a lawyer to defend her and so, after all the prosecution evidence was put forward by Mr Nathan, she had to stand up and address the jury herself. She explained how she had no intention of harming Henry, and with tears running down her cheeks said she would not have done so for all the world. She had just given him a shove to hurry him out of the pub; he had then slipped on the worn steps. She said she had had a lie down for at least two hours before going out, so she could not have been so very tipsy.

Mr Justice Denham was suitably impressed, and advised the jury to acquit Eliza if they thought that she had only used sufficient violence to get her husband out of the pub. This the jury did and the judge discharged her, with a recommendation to keep sober in the future.

Of course if it's a really spectacular bar brawl you're looking for, Elizabeth Mills got one off to a flying start in Leamington Spa in 1830. Elizabeth was the landlady of the *Royal Oak* and wasn't quite the perfect landlady either. For one thing she

Birmingham Law Courts. Author's collection

detested her brother Simon Townsend with a vengeance. Simon had something of a treacherous trait in him and he had given evidence against two of her friends when they were prosecuted for poaching.

Perhaps Simon thought that with Christmas being the season of goodwill and such like, that he would be welcome in the *Royal George* on Boxing Day. He wandered in with the intention of paying some of his workmen their pay. By the time he had got as far as the parlour word had got to Elizabeth. Not surprisingly she refused to serve him any ale.

A few seconds later she came round from the back of the bar clutching a poker.

'You —— rascal, you want to swear some more men's lives away as you did Cottrill and Robbins,' and she started beating him about the head with the poker.

Simon might have thought he was safe when she promptly stormed out of the room, but it was a short lived reprieve. She went into the main bar and returned in a couple of seconds with twenty-two men, all of whom wanted to have a word about his giving evidence. Arthur Tew and George Ludd were the first to

---

ASSAULT AT LEAMINGTON.

John Mills, Elizabeth Mills, Arthur Tew, and *George Ludd,* were indicted for having committed an assault upon Simon Townsend, a painter, of Charlotte-street, in that place, on the 26th of December last.

The Defendant, Mills, keeps the Royal Oak public-house, at Leamington, and the Prosecutor is his wife's brother; the two other Defendants are working men.

The Prosecutor stated, that he went into Mills's house about nine o'clock on the above night, to pay one of his workmen some money, and went into the parlour, when Mrs. Mills came to him, collared him, and struck him violently either with the tongs or poker. She said, " you d—d rascal, you want to swear some more mens' lives away as you did Cotterill's and Robbins's,", (alluding to ———————— some time ago of poaching at

Warwickshire Advertiser

start on him. They punched and kicked him mercilessly, then everyone piled in. Elizabeth's husband got so carried away that he went and got a garden fork, threatening to spill Simon's guts all over the floor.

Simon Townsend struggled against the mass of boots and fists until the whole scrum burst out of the door onto the street. At that point most of his assailants left him lying in the gutter and went back into the warm bar to finish their beer. Tew and Ludd were heard muttering: 'Let's have another go at him,' after bashing his head between the door and door jamb a few times. They then spent the best part of an hour punching and kicking him out in the street.

Eventually they tired of their rather one-sided fight and left him for dead. He managed to survive by the skin of his teeth and several months later managed to bring a prosecution against Elizabeth and John Mills as well as Tew and Ludd. They all got several months hard labour.

The young city of Birmingham had a few pretty ferocious women in it too. In 1848 the area around Beck Lane had become a virtual no go zone for the newly formed police force. It was an area that had been extensively settled by Irish labourers who had their own way of settling their disputes.

On the evening of 18 July the street erupted into one of its periodical riots with a large brawl spilling out of one of the beerhouses. About a dozen men were settling some dispute or other; nobody remembered what started it. On the whole these scraps fizzled out after a while, but this time the police decided to intervene. Once the three officers had got about halfway up the street they were being pelted with stones from every direction. The two sides of the brawl united in an attack on the officers and people poured out of houses for hundreds of yards around to have a go at them too. It was a classic scrap. PC William Toney went down under the furious assault, PC John Simpson and PC Joseph Matthews managed to struggle out and raise the alarm, more officers rushed to their assistance and eventually overwhelm the mob. Some dozen people were arrested of whom Susan Cody was one. She had distinguished herself by jumping up and down on William Toney until he was pounded to pulp. He barely survived and was unable to walk for months afterwards. Margaret Kelly was arrested as well, but there was no definite evidence on which to find her guilty. Susan Cody and all the men were sentenced to six months with hard labour.

If it wasn't drunken brawls that kept the police busy, then it was burglars. In November 1862 there was a regular spate of attempted break-ins around Edgbaston. Most of them were unsuccessful although one house in Calthorpe Street was robbed quite thoroughly. The police arrived just as the burglars were finishing and they escaped with the loot, but had to leave their ladder behind. The villains weren't having much success and matters were about to get worse. They made the mistake of choosing Mrs Bellamy's house in Summer Street for their next target. Mrs Bellamy was no shrinking violet.

On Friday 21 November, Mrs Bellamy went to bed at about ten as usual. At one in the morning she was woken up by the sounds of voices in her front garden. She opened the window and spotted two men lurking in the shadows of the shrubbery. She called out to them and demanded to know what they wanted. The two men kept their heads down and made no reply. Mrs Bellamy was having none of this and went back into her bedroom, loaded a pistol, came back to the window and promptly fired it at them. The two men left at considerable speed, and kept running. The spate of burglaries came to an end that night. Quite what would have happened to Mrs Bellamy if she hadn't taken a pot shot at them is an open question. As dawn broke Constable Whitley searched the garden and found a mask, a gimlet (a very nasty narrow bladed knife) and a razor lying on the ground. The men had been equipped for some serious violence.

CHAPTER 14

Infant Deaths: Sarah Hood and Others

MANCETTER AND BIRMINGHAM

1874–99

She still referred to the child as 'it' . . .

A recurring theme of the Victorian period was that of alcoholic ruin. The perils of the bottle were highlighted at almost every possible opportunity. Drug abuse whether alcohol or opium was rife, and given the squalid conditions of working-class life it isn't surprising. The mill towns of the north had a reputation for using laudanum to make the incessantly repetitive tasks in the mills bearable. In rural Warwickshire it was to the bottle of booze that the depressed turned when every thing else went wrong.

Sarah Hood was a fairly typical case. She was a twenty-eight-year-old dressmaker living in Mancetter. Working in the textile industries in Victorian times was enough to turn a saint to drink. The hours were long and the pay pathetic. Sarah Hood managed to get herself pregnant and on 13 March 1873 gave birth to a baby boy who was christened William. There was no sign of the father, so she was forced to look after the child alone.

Sarah Hood was far from a naturally gifted mother. She seems to have resented and rejected the child from its first breath. William appears to have been a perfectly normal and healthy boy of normal weight. Her neighbours however were stunned to hear her refer to the child as a thing. As the months passed they became more concerned at Sarah's behaviour, and the failure of the baby to thrive. When they managed to find Sarah sober enough to talk, they told her to buck her ideas up and look after the child better. Sarah told them to mind their own business; the child was hers to do with as she pleased.

Not many more months passed before the neighbours called in the relieving officer of the local workhouse. The baby was taken away from Sarah and examined. William was terribly hungry and guzzled his milk voraciously, but there was nothing else wrong him. After a few days he was returned to Sarah with a stern injunction to feed him properly and keep him washed.

A few more months passed, by now William was a regular visitor to the workhouse doctor. Sarah kept telling Dr Handford that William was sick and each time the doctor carefully examined the child and found nothing wrong apart from hunger and neglect. He eventually cautioned her that she would get into trouble if she didn't start looking after the child properly. She still referred to the child as 'it' and showed no interest in the infant's welfare. Sarah continued to drink heavily.

The wheels of Victorian welfare turned very slowly. Eventually the child would be taken from Sarah and raised in the workhouse. Sarah in turn would have been prosecuted for neglecting her child. Unfortunately nature took its course far faster. On 26 July 1874 Sarah woke up to find William dead in his cot. She called another local woman in to help, but William was long past helping, he had been dead for hours. Dr Handford was called and he certified death. The coroner, Mr Thomas Dowes, was informed and he insisted on a post-mortem.

The inquest, held on Wednesday 29 July at the *Dolphin Inn*, saw Sarah Hood arrested on a charge of manslaughter and sent to Warwick Gaol. The post-mortem revealed that William had been systematically starved to death. Although he bore no signs of violence and his organs were perfectly healthy, he weighed only four and a half pounds – less than when he was born. The doctor had searched Sarah's house and found some flour in the cupboard but Sarah had been too drunk to be able to do anything with it.

Sarah languished in Warwick Gaol until 19 December. She had been found guilty of manslaughter at the quarter sessions and sentenced to ten years penal servitude.

Mary Jane Onslow was another similar character.

Harry Onslow worked as a warehouseman at the Battery Company Works in Selly Oak, leaving home at four in the morning and not usually returning until after nine at night, six days a week. Mary Onslow might have had a husband, but with those working hours it was pretty academic. Harry never gave

THE MANCETTER STARVING CASE.—*Sarah Hood*, 28, dressmaker, who was found guilty yesterday of the manslaughter of her illegitimate child, William Hood, at Mancetter, on the 26th July, was brought up to receive sentence. — His lordship told the prisoner she had been found guilty on very clear testimony of causing the death of her child by criminal neglect. He could not conceive a case which more fully illustrated the horrors of habitual intoxication. She seemed to have been one of those wicked persons who allowed self-indulgence in strong drink to overcome all feelings of humanity towards her offspring. The child was proved to have been a healthy infant, and one to all appearance which would have lived to that day had it not been for her neglect. When repeatedly warned of the consequences of her conduct, she referred to her offspring as a piece of inanimate property, and made use of the unnatural expression that she could do as she liked with her own. On the other hand, there was evidence that there was corn flour in the house, but this provision was rendered useless by the habitual state of intoxication in which she was proved to spend her time. The sentence would be ten years' penal servitude.

Warwickshire Advertiser

her any housekeeping money because he knew she would be straight down to the pub with it. They lived in one furnished room in one of the squalid courts at the back of Allison Street, Birmingham.

Mary Jane Onlsow was well known to the local Inspector for the Society for Prevention of Cruelty to Children. He had called round frequently in 1899 trying to persuade Mary to take better care of her children. The youngest daughter, Agnes May, was twenty months old but she was barely half her normal weight. Priscilla Kay, a neighbour saw Agnes left in the yard all day, dressed in one tatty garment. The child was dumped in the yard again the next day and Priscilla called in the inspector.

Mary went on drinking binges. The inspector called again in August and found the children alone in the dingy room. When he asked where their mother was, the two boys took him round to the *British Lion Inn*. There he found her thoroughly drunk and got a torrent of abuse for his concern. All the children were dirty, starved and the room was utterly filthy. Mary went on another bender during the August Bank Holiday. She was so drunk that she fell over in the street. The children were placed in the workhouse while she recovered.

Inspector Holmes called on 7 September to find the children still no better treated and Mary slumped in a chair, half-dressed and sporting a black eye. He found that Agnes was dressed in only a couple of rags. He asked Mary how this state of affairs came about but she shrugged and said they were perfectly alright. Mrs Cave, the landlady, snorted with derision: 'The reason why they are so neglected is that you are always drinking.'

Mary's neighbours were heartily sick of her. Kate Clark had taken Agnes into her home and cared for her when Mary went out on a two-day bender. Leah Terry had done much the same. The day before the inspectors visit, their patience finally ran out and all the women of the court grabbed Mary and gave her a traditional ducking in the horse trough.

The ducking brought about an improvement. For a few weeks Mary looked after the children reasonably well, but for little Agnes it was not enough to remedy the long-term starvation. On 1 October Mary took Agnes to Dr Murphy, who prescribed some medicine to be taken with milk and port wine. Maybe it was the thought of the port wine; Mary went off on another drinking binge for three days. Kate Clark, Rose Lee and the others did what they could for the children out of pity, but they had little to share. It was now 5 October and the children needed warmth as well as sustenance.

Rose Lee sent her daughter Agnes up to the Onslow's room with some food and drink. Agnes found the little mite moaning in pain and called her mother for help. They tried to settle her and hoped that Harry would come home from work soon.

Harry got back from work at nine-thirty. He found Agnes May dead on the bed. She was just twenty-two months old and had starved to death because of the neglect of her mother.

Drink was not the only cause of infanticide, locked into an endless cycle of poverty and suffering some women went mad. The appalling housing conditions that drove Mary Onslow to the bottle had, some years earlier, pushed Mary Ann Horsfall over the edge of madness. In a world where there was no health care at all the tragedy was almost inevitable.

Mary Ann married Joseph Thomas Horsfall in 1871 and, as was the case in those days, started a large family; by 1891 she had brought nine children into the world. It had not been easy. In April 1883 one of her children died and she took it very hard. The following year she attempted to commit suicide by taking rat poison, but her husband had managed to save her. In the following years she tried jumping out of an upstairs window and then cutting her wrists. Luckily her elder daughters managed to stop her both times.

Life was not to get any better at all. In November 1890 one of her sons drowned. She was now forty years old, heavily pregnant and utterly depressed. Sarah Ann Matts came and sat in with her as her labour drew near. The family was so poor that the cost of a doctor or even a midwife was simply out of the question. Sarah listened to Mary moaning that she wished she were dead and that the expected new baby was already in heaven with the drowned boy. Mary Ann's last confinement was in the dirty cold bedroom that served the whole family. After the birth she started to drink heavily.

On the second Saturday of April her son, Joseph, came back from Coventry to see how his parents were getting on. He was startled to discover that his mother did not seem to recognise him. She was in a distracted mood and wandered about the house. On the Sunday morning Mr Horsfall bought a bottle of port wine to celebrate his son coming home. Mary refused to drink it until someone else had tasted it, she was under the delusion that it might be poisoned. She picked up a broom and went upstairs to sweep the bedroom. After ten minutes father and son heard her cry out: 'Oh Joe, I've killed the baby.'

Joseph raced up the stairs to the bedroom and saw to his utter horror that Mary was swinging the baby's head against the bedpost. He managed to grab the child from her before she could do it again. He handed the baby to his father and restrained her. Mr Horsfall cradled his tiny son in his arms hoping he was alright. It was not to be, within moments the little baby had died.

Neighbours and the police were soon on the scene. The doctor discovered that the child's skull had suffered a massive depressed fracture that had caused almost instant death. Mary admitted that she had done it, and so she was charged with wilful murder at the inquest. She ended her days in an asylum.

CHILD MURDER IN BIRMINGHAM.

Mr. B. Weekes (Deputy-Coroner) held an inquest at the Coroner's Court, Moor Street, on Tuesday, on the body of the male infant of Joseph Thomas Horsfall, who was murdered by his mother, Mary Ann Horsfall, aged 40, on Sunday morning at her residence, 5 Court, 4 house, Bartholomew Row. The mother, who was in Court in charge of Detective Monk, was defended by Mr. Peet.—Joseph Thomas Horsfall, the father of the child, said his wife had had nine children. An inquest was held on one boy in November last, who died from drowning, An inquest was also held in April, 1883, on a child which was found dead in bed. His wife had not been sound in her mind since losing the child in 1883. Since the death of the one in November she had troubled a great deal and taken to drink. Only a neighbour had attended her in her last confinement, and ever since she had been very ill and

Warwickshire Advertiser

CHAPTER 15

More Suspicious Infant Deaths

EATINGTON AND ASTON

1874–88

The court case was a closely argued one.

Patience Spencer ended up on a charge of wilful murder on 9 July 1874 alongside her husband, Charles. The case was to reveal the true cost of the agricultural depression that had plagued the country for a decade. This case was not for the faint hearted, then or now, as it shows the desperate conditions of the rural labourers and the lengths that some of them felt they had to go to. There were horror stories about what happened in the countryside, but not even the judge was fully prepared for the real facts.

Charles Spencer was thirty-two and, by all accounts, not too bright. Nevertheless he had married twenty-five-year-old Patience in the April of 1874. She was very obviously pregnant at the time and the couple had moved into one of the labourer's cottages in the village of Halford. The two of them worked on Lambcott Farm, which was run by Mrs Mann. In those days a pregnant woman worked to within days of her confinement, and was back at work just as soon as physically possible. Even so, on 21 May their neighbour Mary Ann Southam suggested that Patience stay at home, she was in that much distress trying to work when so heavily pregnant. Mary Southam and her husband Richard also worked on the farm. Patience told Mary that she didn't think her time was so near. Patience continued to work; it was the season for hoeing the bean crop, chopping up all the annual weeds to give the beans plenty of light to grow.

On 11 June Patience, Charles and another labourer by the name of Benjamin Webb were hoeing the beans in one field, there were some more women working in an adjoining field and a man working in yet another field nearby. At about ten o'clock Patience dropped her hoe and went to the ditch at the bottom

of the field. There she lay moaning in pain. At intervals Charles
went over to see if she was alright, but returned to carry on with
his work. This went on all morning until they broke for lunch
at one. Patience struggled out of the ditch and sat with Richard
and Charles, sipping some tea that Charles had brought with
him. She was in a dreadful state, moaning in pain and unable
to rest.

After their lunch break Richard Webb had to get on with his
hoeing. Patience struggled up the field, helped by Charles, until
they reached the shade of an ash bush. Richard glanced at them
occasionally during the afternoon. He saw her lying down with
her skirts raised, and Charles tending to her. At four o'clock
Charles left her and didn't return until half five. At six Richard
finished work for the day and walked home, passing Charles
Spencer at the top of the field. Charles was cutting a fagot of
wood with his knife. Richard was deeply alarmed at the sight of
Charles' hands; they were covered in blood.

Richard fretted through the night about what he should do.
The following morning he persuaded Thomas Ball to go with
him to look at the ash bush. They found a large pool of congealed
blood hastily covered over with soil. Seriously worried, they
called over the farm bailiff, William Bird. He found a second
concealed pool of blood on the other side of the bush.

The local constable, Charles Hart, was informed on Saturday
13th and on Sunday the 14th he, together with Constable Oliver
Crook, went to the Spencer's house in Halford.

Charles Spencer asked what the constable wanted and
Charles Hart said he had heard that his wife had been confined
of a child. Spencer replied he didn't know what he meant. The
constable then asked if he could see Spencer's knife. Spencer
produced it, realising that the truth was out. When Charles Hart
then asked where the baby was, Spencer said that it was in a pit
on the farm. The constable asked if he would take him there and
Charles readily agreed. The two of them went off on their grim
errand, leaving PC Oliver Crook with Patience.

Charles Spencer led the constable first to the ash bush where
the delivery had taken place. The officer asked if the baby was a
boy or girl, and Charles said it was a lad. He was then asked if
the baby was alive, Charles replying: 'Yes. I killed it and put it in
the ditch, where it stopped till night. Then I took it and threw it

into the middle of the pit.'

By now they had reached the pit and Constable Hart pulled off his trousers to wade into the water to try and find the body. He eventually found it and realised there were several knife wounds on the child. He cautioned Charles Spencer. Charles told him: 'I did it; it's a bad job. I would not have had it happen for a hundred pounds.'

Back at the Spencer's cottage, Constable Crook was talking to Patience. He had heard Charles say the baby was in the pit and asked her who had killed the child. She told him that it was her husband, but that she wished it had never happened for all the world. She insisted that it was her husband that had delivered her and that she was unconscious for the latter part of the delivery.

The next day Superintendent Thompson took them to Shipston police station and the body of the child sent for a post-mortem. It was to reveal that the child had three deep knife wounds, but the doctors could not agree whether he was alive when they were inflicted. In fact they couldn't be sure if the child had ever had an independent existence. The one doctor felt fairly sure that it had, and that was enough to get both of

THE CHARGE OF WILFUL MURDER AT EATINGTON.—*Charles* and *Patience Spencer*, agricultural labourer and his wife, were placed in the dock and called upon to plead for having murdered a certain male infant child, recently born of the body of the female prisoner, at Eatington, on the 11th June.—In reply to the clerk of arraigns, the male prisoner pleaded guilty.—His lordship asked him if he clearly understood the nature of his answer. The charge was for having deliberately and purposely destroyed the life of his child. He did not wish to resist the plea, if the prisoner felt he was really guilty, but he must tell him that his life was the forfeit.—The male prisoner began to cry, and said he did not understand and wished to get pardoned.—After further telling the prisoner that, if he still adhered to the plea of guilty, the sentence of the Court would be that he be hanged by the neck until he was dead, the prisoner, in reply to the governor of the gaol, submitted the plea of not guilty, and his lordship assigned two counsel to defend both him and his wife, and directed that they be put on their trial to-morrow morning.

Warwickshire Advertiser

them charged with wilful murder.

The court case was a closely argued one. Patience insisted that she had passed out before the child was born and was not aware of what had happened. The prosecution finally accepted this and the judge directed the jury to find Patience not guilty, and she was acquitted. Charles, however, was found guilty of concealing a birth. The evidence surrounding the cause of the child's death was too conflicting to prove murder or manslaughter. Charles was sentenced to eighteen months hard labour.

Life and death in the Victorian countryside could be ruthlessly cruel and callous, the poor woman had spent all day in labour, with no one coming to her assistance apart from her clumsy husband who may well have killed the child in a cack handed attempt to save his wife's life during a breech birth. It was all a long way away from the Country Diary of an Edwardian Lady.

Of course you didn't have to live in the countryside to conceal a birth and a case in Aston during 1888 shows just how different life could be in the city.

Elizabeth Cheshire was charged with wilfully and with malice afore thought murdering her illegitimate female child. Elizabeth was a twenty-year-old pressworker when she sought lodgings from Mrs Francis Thomson on 19 August 1887. The house in New Road, Aston was rather overcrowded. Elizabeth's brother shared a room with some other men in one part of the house and Elizabeth shared a room with two other young women. There was just the one bed for them all to sleep in and despite privacy being something of a rare commodity in the household, neither of the two girls seemed to notice that Elizabeth was pregnant.

Mrs Thomson had noticed she was getting rather stout, and asked her about it. Elizabeth denied that she was pregnant, although Mrs Thomson wasn't exactly convinced, she was old enough to spot the signs. As autumn passed into winter Elizabeth got even stouter. You would have thought that Ellen Figure and Miss Thomas would have said something about the rapidly diminishing amount of room in the bed, but Christmas came and went without any alarms.

Late on the night of 30 December the three girls were all

asleep in the bed. The room was pitch dark; little light filtered in through the window as the street lighting in Aston was patchy and insignificant. Ellen Figure heard Elizabeth get out of bed sometime in the night. Miss Thomas woke up too. They heard what they thought was Elizabeth being sick and Ellen asked what was the matter. In the darkness, Elizabeth told them she was alright, just a bit sick. Ellen asked if she should light the candle but Elizabeth said no, she would be back in bed in a few minutes. A short while later she got back into the bed and the three of them drifted back off to sleep.

As the first hint of dawn crept across the room Ellen woke once more. Elizabeth was not in bed; Ellen could hear someone going down stairs and shuffling about. She drifted back off to sleep again. A little later they all got up, but Ellen was pretty ill and went back to sleep as the other two girls went off to work. On their way they mentioned the night's events to Mrs Thomson. She brought a cup of tea up to Elizabeth and no doubt had a good nose around. The floor of the room was damp.

Elizabeth revived with the cup of tea and came downstairs. She took a pail of water up to the room and cleaned the floor, then came back downstairs to the parlour and lay on the sofa. Three times during the afternoon she fainted, but each time denied anything was seriously wrong. Mrs Thomson wasn't that daft and knew something had happened, but she wasn't entirely certain what it was. The next day was a Sunday and Elizabeth spent the day resting.

The following day, 2 January 1888, Elizabeth Cheshire was well enough to go back to work. She appeared in good spirits and perfectly healthy. At midday Mrs Thomson decided she would search Elizabeth's box of belongings, she was sure something had gone on. She was quite right, inside the trunk she found some bloodstained rags and then her worst fears were realised as she unwrapped a skirt to find the body of a newborn girl. It had a handkerchief knotted around its neck. She sat there in the bedroom stunned and unsure what to do next. She found Elizabeth's brother still in his room and showed him the body.

Elizabeth returned for her dinner shortly afterwards. Mrs Thomson pointed at the trunk and demanded an explanation.

'I didn't mean to do it Mrs Thomson, I am going home this afternoon and I will take it with me.'

Mrs Thomson was having none of this. She sent another lodger to get a policeman and within in minutes PC Dawson arrived. He found Elizabeth in floods of tears, swearing she had not killed the child. He charged her with murder but she burst out again: 'I did not kill it.' PC Russell had also come along, he checked the body and found the handkerchief knotted around its neck. PC Dawson also charged Elizabeth with concealing the birth of a child, and she was taken to the police station.

'Someone else shall suffer for this beside me,' she stated when questioned in the cells. When the officer asked what she meant she referred to 'a chap named Drinkwater'. Presumably this was the father who had dumped her when the results of his attentions became obvious.

The local doctor, Dr Bark examined the baby and performed a post-mortem. When the matter came to court it was his evidence that would be crucial to the charge. If the child had lived and breathed on its own, then Elizabeth would have been guilty of wilful murder and probably been sentenced to death. If, however, the child had never had an independent life then Elizabeth would only have been guilty of concealing the birth; a serious offence but not a capital one.

The case came to court on 18 January. The two girls who

ALLEGED CHILD MURDER AT ASTON: THE JUDGE AND THE MEDICAL WITNESS.—*Elizabeth Cheshire*, 20, pressworker, was charged with having, on the 30th December last, at Aston, wilfully and of malice aforethought murdered her illegitimate female child ; and on a second indictment with having unlawfully endeavoured to conceal the birth of that child by a secret disposition of the dead body.—Mr. Soden, assisted by Mr. Colmore, appeared for the prosecution, and Mr. Hugo Young defended.—Mr. Soden, in opening the case, said the prisoner at the bar was charged with the murder of her illegitimate child, at Aston, on the 30th December last. What was alleged against the

Warwickshire Advertiser

shared a bed with Elizabeth on that fateful night gave their evidence. Neither of them had heard a child cry, only the sounds of Elizabeth apparently being sick. Dr Bark was called to give his evidence and was almost immediately censured by the judge for giving his evidence in a supercilious manner, smirking and smiling about the nature of the post-mortem. By the time Dr Bark had finished his testimony the judge was absolutely furious and gave him the most withering criticism short of prosecuting him for contempt of court. Dr Bark had originally stated that the handkerchief around the baby's neck may well have been an aid to pulling it out as Elizabeth struggled to give birth alone, but then he changed his evidence to state that this was impossible. He did, however, state that the child's lungs were not fully inflated and so may never have completed its first breath. Elizabeth Cheshire then fainted in the dock.

The jury found her not guilty of murder, but guilty of concealing the birth, and for this she was sentenced to six months hard labour. As though she hadn't had a hard enough labour already.

CHAPTER 16

A Sensational Elopement

LEAMINGTON SPA

1888

*Ada opened the bedroom window, dropped her
suitcase to her lover, and shinned down the
drainpipe into his warm embrace.*

Researching all these grim tales can be pretty heavy
going. Page after eye-watering page of Victorian
newspapers, week by week for a whole century, con-
centrating on the ghastly consequences of human
frailty is a pretty depressing affair, and I presume that reading
these tales can get a bit gloomy too. But every now and then a
tale appears that raises a chuckle. This one has neither foul nor
suspicious deaths, and had everyone in the record office in fits
of laughter. There was some 'unpleasantness' involved, as the
newspaper accounts of 28 April 1888 reported, and that's a
good enough excuse for me to include the story in this book.

Ada Lucy Hanbury Williams was the very wealthy
daughter of the even wealthier Ferdinand Capel Hanbury
Williams, who owned a vast amount of land around
Abergavenney. Occasionally, the family stayed in Leamington
to take the waters. The Pump Rooms were a popular
destination with wealthy families and their trade was one of
the factors in the town's rise to fame. Victorian matrons
promenaded up and down the parade, all fiercely jealous of
their social status. Older businessmen took the waters in the
hope of curing their gout, and conducting deals on the side.
The social order of the day was very rigid and the upper
classes rarely even noticed the presence of the ordinary
factory workers or servants. The upstairs, downstairs culture
was at its height. Ada, who was twenty-four in 1888, had led
a typically sheltered life on the enormous estate in Wales and
considered the trips to Leamington to be a brief glimpse of

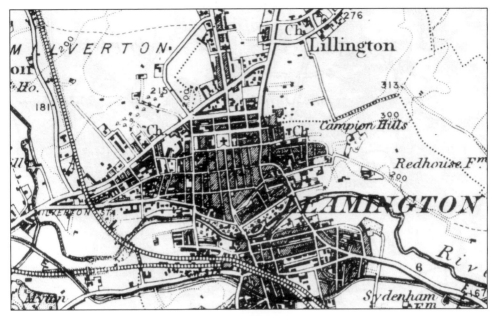

Victorian Leamington Spa. Author's collection

the social high life. The newspapers described her as about
five feet six tall, with a fair complexion and was 'tolerably
good looking'. It was in Leamington that she met the love of
her life, and fell headlong into a passionate infatuation - much
to the annoyance of her father.

James Albert Levey was groom in the service of Mr Sewell at
Elmshurst. He was just nineteen, a couple of inches shorter than
Ada and of a 'moderate' build. His family lived in a little cottage
in Cubbington. In those days Cubbington was not so much of a
suburb of the town as a village in its own right, and considered
rather old fashioned too. James' father, Charles, was a
foundryman at Flavell's and his family was quite definitely an
ordinary working-class one. James even had a girl friend, Alice
Wright, who was a domestic servant, a cook, at Colonel
Magrath's house in Clarendon Square. James and Alice were
due to get married and in April. Alice had handed in her notice
in preparation for her marriage at the end of the month. But
James had fallen passionately in love by then, and not with her.

Quite how James Levey, the groom, and Ada Williams, the
heiress, met in the first place has not been recorded. Their

ardent romance soon came to the notice of Ada's father and he was not in the least impressed. He forcibly threw James out of the house. He then packed Ada off to the family mansion with instructions for her to be kept there and to have no more to do with the entirely unsuitable James Levey. The two lovers managed to keep in touch. Ada smuggled letters out of the mansion and told James where she was being held prisoner. It seems he managed to get secret letters to her under the nose of the governess. Ada was good friends with the local postmaster. A plot worthy of Shakespeare was being hatched.

In mid-April James took the train down to the family mansion and presented himself at the door as her rich cousin from the Midlands. The staff were deceived and Ada and James were allowed to meet. They planned their next move under the noses of the people who were supposed to be keeping Ada incommunicado. They only had a few minutes alone, but that was enough. James was given a guest bedroom on the far side of the house. But in the middle of the night James was not in bed; he was waiting on the lawn. Ada opened her bedroom window, dropped her suitcase to her lover, and shinned down the drainpipe into his warm embrace. Quickly they made their way to the station and were soon on the way back to Leamington.

The next morning the alarm was raised when neither of the lovebirds turned up for breakfast. The staff started searching the area for any sign of the 'rich cousin' and Ada. It was all a bit late, the couple had already got back to James' family home in Cubbington, and James had booked a special wedding licence with the registrar in Bedford Street. They took a cab to the office at ten-thirty and by eleven were man and wife. It was a sensation, plenty of James' friends knew what was going on and by midday the couple had returned to Cubbington for a marathon wedding celebration. The whole village thought it was grand fun, the affair even got into the local papers.

Of course Alice Wright wasn't quite so impressed. The next day she got two nasty surprises. The first was seeing her fiancé in all the papers for marrying some one else. The second shock, and the one that really got her irate, was getting a piece of the wedding cake. Just about spitting blood, she stormed over to Cubbington to tell James exactly what she thought of him. She managed to catch James' mum on the doorstep as she was carrying out a bucket of slops. Words were exchanged, rather heated ones. James' mum threatened to chuck the slops over her head. Alice returned to Leamington and saw a lawyer. In Cubbington the celebrations continued for the next week. Old Mr Levey was reported as saying: 'He ain't going to work now as his son has married an heiress.'

Alas, history does not record whether they all lived happily ever after. I hope so.

LEAMINGTON GAZETTE.

SENSATIONAL ELOPEMENT AND MARRIAGE AT LEAMINGTON.

THE GROOM AND THE HEIRESS!.

"The course of true love never did run smooth," but the young Cubbington groom and the heiress of Abergavenny have put an end to the many obstacles which confronted them by becoming man and wife. It generally follows that when a young lady, who is the fortunate possessor of a large fortune, falls in love with a young man who is poor, but honest, there are decided objections to the union by the lady's acquaintances, and so it happened in the present instance. Of course, according to all the common usages of society, the objections on the part of the lady's parents were perfectly natural, but neither she nor her lover looked upon the matter in quite the same light. As the one had sufficient income to keep both, they saw no earthly reason why they should not take each other "for better, for worse," and they at once proceeded to carry out their plans, which have resulted in the complete discomfiture of those who were strenuously opposed to the union. And on this hangs a tale.

protesta
for Mr.
the repo
that "t
followin
The onl
the nar
parents,
boys, a
fashione
of roma
cottage
Levy pl
the mor
yet they
These
problem
Jehu p
tion. T
with he
omnibus
a startli
made b
significa
did ever

CHAPTER 17

Poisoned by Sarah Kibler

LEAMINGTON SPA

1889

*Within an hour her mouth had become
swollen and inflamed.*

D r Horniblow and his wife, Elizabeth, lived in Clarendon Terrace, Leamington Spa in 1889. They were of fairly mature years and had just one child, William Henry, who was a lad of fourteen. Dr Horniblow was considered a little bit eccentric because he followed the philosophy and poetry of Matthew Arnold. The latter was an early Victorian poet who rejected the classical dogmas of the Christian Church in favour of a rather looser definition of God as a kind of Time Spirit. By 1889 this rejection of formal christianity had been crystallised into agnosticism. The Agnostics believed that the belief in God was not rational and that God could not be proved rationally as a result. They did not reject the possibility of God, but thought that mankind could cope quite happily on its own. Perhaps Dr Horniblow had seen enough of the random illnesses that struck down rich and poor, good and evil alike to feel that God had forsaken humanity, simply didn't care, or didn't exist. His agnostic beliefs were a direct challenge to the established social order of the middle classes of Victorian England. It was these beliefs that would prevent him from seeking the help that he needed. Despite his rather odd beliefs Doctor Horniblow was a good doctor who tended to the needs of his patients rather better than some of the other local medical men. In spite of this his wife became very ill in February of this year and took to her bed.

The good doctor didn't believe in having a flock of domestic servants around the house in the way that most households of his status did. They had just one charwoman, Sarah Kibler. She was no spring chicken herself and probably found that keeping the place tidy in just a couple of hours a day was very hard work. When Elizabeth Horniblow became ill and confined to bed Sarah was taken on as a full-time servant for a few months. She had much the same cleaning duties as before, the rooms downstairs, the bedrooms and the doctors consulting room upstairs, and a few meals to cook as well. She had to attend on Mrs Horniblow as she lay recuperating in her room upstairs. The contemporary accounts show Mrs Horniblow as a fairly weak character, doting on her husband and child, almost certainly reading poetry about nature's wonders and spoiling her pet rat to the point where even her husband had had enough of the wretched thing.

Sarah Kibler found that the new hours were an altogether more satisfactory arrangement. She was getting much better wages, more food and job security. There were drawbacks of course, but nothing that couldn't be sorted out. Sarah was a devious sort of character and started plotting to secure her

Clarendon Square and Place, home to the professionals of Leamington.

The author

employment in a rather unusual way. The contents of the doctor's surgery gave her a few ideas.

Dr Horniblow had to go away on 7 March. Mrs Horniblow stayed in bed, gradually getting her strength back. Sarah Kibler cleaned the house as usual that morning and, for the first time, she cleaned the consulting room without Mrs Horniblow. Inside the room were arranged various medicines and poisons on the shelves. One particular bottle was labelled 'Corrosive Sublimate' and 'POISON'. It was a particularly vicious chemical, Mercuric Chloride, minute doses of which were used to cure syphilis (although the 'cure' often killed the patient). In the afternoon she took Mrs Horniblow her tea as usual. Sarah Kibler was somewhat annoyed about this little ritual. Elizabeth Horniblow had a pet rat. It was allowed to come out of its cage, sit on the tea tray and, whilst Elizabeth sat up, the little white rat with its beady pink eyes would run around the bed and tea tray. Elizabeth simply adored the creature and would hear nothing said against it. Sarah Kibler thought it was a rat, and should be treated like any other of the bald-tailed vermin.

After only a couple of sips of the tea Mrs Horniblow spat it out. It tasted simply dreadful, a mixture of Lucifer Matches and copper, she said. Within an hour she was doubled up in agony and vomiting blood. Sarah took the tea things downstairs and washed them up. Dr Horniblow got back to the house at four o'clock and immediately administered some Castor Oil to his wife. He had no idea what was wrong with her, but the Castor Oil seemed to help and she stopped being sick. It was all a bit of a mystery – perhaps it was something to do with the illness that had confined her to bed three weeks earlier.

Elizabeth was talking to Sarah some while later: 'I'm so glad I didn't die, I don't know what my husband and little boy would have done without me.'

Sarah told her that they would have done quite well; Sarah would have cooked and cleaned for them whilst her husband could have looked after the garden and done the boots. It probably wasn't the most tactful way of putting it, but it certainly expressed Sarah's ambitions very succinctly.

Sarah continued to do the housework and cooking. A week later she took a plate of kidneys up to Mrs Horniblow for her supper. As usual the rat was sitting on her dinner tray and playing around the bedroom. Mrs Horniblow wasn't feeling up to eating the kidneys; her stomach was still rather delicate after the mysterious illness of the week before. The untouched kidneys were taken back down to the kitchen and then chucked out into the garden for the next door neighbours cat to promptly devour.

The next day the neighbours asked Dr Horniblow to have a look at their cat and try to work out why it had died. He couldn't really find an obvious reason. The poor thing had a dreadfully swollen stomach, but no signs of damage; a cart hadn't run it down. It was all very odd.

The next major tragedy was on 18 March. Elizabeth Horniblow was devastated by the death of her dear little pet rat. The thing was found in its cage, stomach horribly swollen. Amid floods of tears, the much loved rodent was cremated on

The doctor's surgery contained nearly as many chemicals as a druggists shop, and the difference between most medicines and most poisons is simply a matter of dose.

The author

the kitchen fire. Dr Horniblow may well have had a vague love of all things natural, a sympathy with Wordsworth and the other romantic poets; but that rat went straight onto the fire. Elizabeth was recovering from her illness, but set back by this emotional catastrophe. She retired back to bed. Sarah Kibler carried on with the domestic duties, but Dr Horniblow was starting to get concerned at these strange deaths.

Elizabeth managed to get up and about a few days later, much recovered. On 21 March she even managed to walk into the town centre for a bit of exercise. Joseph Bellamy, the milkman, was pleased but very surprised to see her fit and healthy again. Only the previous day Sarah Kibler had told him that Elizabeth had the mark of death upon her, how she had heard death's footsteps in the house when no one else was about. Sarah had told him that she thought Elizabeth would be dead inside a week. All very creepy thought Joseph, so he was thoroughly shocked to see Elizabeth promenading down the Parade.

Two days later, on the 23rd, Elizabeth was feeling even better. She was in the kitchen making herself a glass of brandy and warm water. She put the cup down on the table to let it cool. It was a warm spring afternoon, the garden beckoned and she went out to see how the bulbs and spring flowers were coming on. After about ten minutes she went back into the kitchen. Sarah was fussing about the sink and William, her son, was there too. She picked up the cup of brandy and took a sip. Revolted at the taste, she spat it out. It tasted exactly the same as the cup of tea that had made her so ill a few weeks ago and she said so in no uncertain terms.

Sarah Kibler quickly crossed the kitchen to the table and snatched the tablecloth off. The cup fell to the floor and smashed. Sarah quickly cleaned up the mess and threw the broken bits of the cup into the ash pit. Elizabeth may have been pleased that she was so quick to clear up the mess, at this juncture she didn't think that there was any ulterior motive for the accidental breaking and disposal of the cup. Within an hour her mouth had become swollen and inflamed. Luckily she had not swallowed any of the drink.

Dr Horniblow was slowly putting two and two together. Still, with Elizabeth up and about again he could at least dispense with the expense of a full time charwoman, and on 6 April her

The doctor would have been better to have gone straight to the police rather than try to lay down the law himself. Strand Magazine

term of service expired and he informed her that he no longer needed her services. Quite how much he suspected at this stage is not known. In his surgery the contents of one of the bottles had mysteriously shrunk. It was the bottle of Corrosive Sublimate. He started to investigate.

William Henry went through the contents of the ash pit and found the fragments of the brandy cup. The doctor performed some chemical tests on it and found that there was a thick residue of Corrosive Sublimate on the bottom of the cup. He decided to have the matter out with Sarah and summoned her to an interview. He should have gone straight to the magistrates or police, but his agnostic religious views had threatened and aggravated them; he felt he had to manage this affair on his own.

On 27 April Sarah and her husband turned up at his house. Dr Horniblow produced the bottle of poison and accused her of poisoning the rat and his wife. Mr Kibler told his wife that she must confess to what she had done. Sarah burst into floods of tears and begged forgiveness.

He glowered at her sternly, saying: 'Now you ——- old hag, ask Mrs Horniblow to forgive you.'

Sarah went into Mrs Horniblow and once again begged for forgiveness. Mrs Horniblow seems to have been under the impression that Sarah had only poisoned the rat. She forgave her. Dr Horniblow was not finished with Sarah Kibler yet though. He demanded that she leave town by the end of the week and never return to Leamington again. He did not intend to involve the police with the matter.

Of course, Sarah Kibler and her husband couldn't just up sticks and leave town. On their income it just was not an option. They stayed and Dr Horniblow felt that this was a personal affront to him. He had no option but to place the affair in the hands of the local magistrates. On 1 May the Warwick magistrates heard the case. They were quite concerned that Dr Horniblow refused to take the oath on the Bible when giving his evidence. As a follower of Matthew Arnold he considered this to be superstitious nonsense and wouldn't stoop to such a charade. Another concern was that the only evidence for the presence of poison was the doctor's own analysis. There was no independent corroboration. The defence lawyer made the most of both these points and the magistrates decided that there was no case for Sarah Kibler to answer. She was discharged from the court. The magistrates made pointed reference to the way his testimony could not be trusted because he would not swear that it was true.

Dr Horniblow was furious. He had been made out to be a buffoon by refusing to take the oath, and possibly a fraud for relying on his own analysis. He immediately sent the fragments of the cup for an independent test by the famous Dr Bostock Hill of Birmingham. His analysis confirmed the presence of the poison and the matter was brought back to court in December.

The next trial was at the Warwickshire Assizes, a far more august court than the magistrates. This time Dr Horniblow did take the oath, and had to explain his change of heart about doing so. Dr Bostock Hill gave his evidence to back up the earlier testimony, and Sarah Kibler was found guilty of trying to murder Mrs Horniblow. She was sentenced to fifteen years penal servitude.

If Sarah Kibler had been a little less generous with the poison it could have had a very different outcome. The evidence in court showed that she had put thirty or forty grains of it in the brandy, enough to kill at least ten people. The poison missing from the bottle was enough to have killed a hundred. Just three grains would have been enough to kill Mrs Horniblow as dead as a doornail. Sarah put so much of the poison in the tea and brandy glass that Elizabeth was promptly sick or spat it out, thus saving her life. A smaller dose would have certainly killed her.

CHAPTER 18

The Mysterious Death
of Hannah Smith
LEAMINGTON SPA
1890

. . . she was up in her room, blind drunk.

Hannah Smith was a spinster and quite a frail sixty-seven year old. She also shared a house with her niece Edith Burbidge. It would be nice to think that the much younger Edith looked after the old lady and the house was a model of Victorian domestic tranquillity. But then it wouldn't be in this book would it? The fact of the matter is that Hannah and Edith got on each others nerves. Hannah was described as 'very tantalising' and Edith was more than a little fond of the odd bottle of brandy, or two. Number 128 Regent Street, Leamington Spa was a fractious household, to put it mildly.

The two women were forever fighting. The neighbours heard it all, and frequently had to call the police to restore some semblance of order. Hannah would call Edith: 'You drunken wretch, you drunken beast' and Edith would retort: 'I will pull your tongue out if you say any more,' and so it went on with Hannah usually ending with the threat: 'You don't want to go to gaol again, you gaol bird.'

Edith had indeed gone to gaol, three times, for assaulting the old lady, and the frequency of their fights was increasing. Edith was first convicted for battering Hannah on 15 January 1887, then again on 23 January 1889 and yet again on the 9 December 1889. By the spring of 1890 matters were far from improving. Pretty much the whole of Regent Street knew of the incessant bickering and occasional explosions of temper. It was generally considered that Edith was a good for nothing drunkard who was simply waiting for Hannah to die so she could spend all the money on brandy. Edith was not popular

Hannah and Edith aggravated each other and their fights were heard by the whole street. Strand Magazine

and her habit of retiring to bed with a few bottles for the whole weekend did little to enhance her reputation. Hannah thought it was utterly disgraceful and said so, long and loud.

In the very early hours of Saturday 15 March PC Rainbow was on patrol in Holly Walk when he heard screams of 'Police!' and 'Break open the door!' He wasn't in the least surprised to find that they were coming from the back of 128 Regent Street. He walked across the road and hammered his fist on the closed shutters. Inside the shouting went quiet and he heard Edith come up to the window. 'Who's there?' she asked. He told her he was a policeman and had heard all the shouting. He then told her that if he heard any more screams from the house he would break open the door and arrest them both. He described Edith's reply as a 'foul expression'. Silence fell over the dark street and PC Rainbow decided it would be politic to let Edith sleep it off rather than tackle this wild-eyed virago.

Saturday morning found Hannah Smith in a very sorry state. Sarah Graves lived in the house next door and often called in to see how Hannah was. She found Hannah had a series of nasty bruises on her wrists and hands. More seriously, she had a couple of head wounds that were giving Hannah a great deal of pain. Hannah sat in the chair in the back room of the shop moaning in agony, muttering: 'Oh my head. Oh my head.' Sarah Graves sent for the doctor.

Dr Horniblow arrived as soon as he could. He examined her hands and found the skin had been knocked off her knuckles in several places. The head wound was deep, but not so deep as to fracture the skull. Hannah was drifting in and out of unconsciousness, so he laid her down on the carpet so that she wouldn't fall off the chair, and hoped that the concussion would wear off, that was about as much as he could do for the old lady. Her wounds didn't seem too serious at first. There was no sign of Edith at all for a while. Later, Sarah found that she was up in her room, blind drunk and decided it would best for everyone if she was left up there undisturbed.

When Dr Horniblow left Sarah Graves went back to her shop and her work as a furrier. After a while she happened to look out of her window and spotted Hannah staggering about in the backyard and eventually fall over onto the brickwork. She rushed around and hauled the old woman back inside. She sent for Dr Horniblow again. He came quickly and tried to make her comfortable. Whilst she was still lucid he asked her what had happened.

Hannah told him that she had gone upstairs that morning and for no apparent reason Edith had suddenly hit her on the head with a pair of coal tongs. Dr Horniblow wasn't convinced that this was the entire story, but he made a note it anyway. He laid her back down onto the rug and told her to rest until he came back later. He wasn't at all happy about her wounds. He returned in the evening to find her semi-conscious and too prostrate to examine her properly. He decided the case was too serious for him to handle alone and sent for Dr Eardley Wilmott for some assistance. Dr Wilmott arrived shortly after midnight and Sarah Graves lost no time in telling him that Edith had knocked Hannah about when she was drunk.

On Sunday morning Hannah's sister, Mary, arrived. Hannah was still awake, rocking from side to side moaning about the pain in her head. Mary called out: 'Oh, Hannah, Hannah, what is the matter?' Hannah replied: 'She did it. She did it.'

'Where did you get that blow?'

'She thumped my head on the floor.'

It may be that she was getting confused and had muddled up the fall in the yard with an attack by Edith. There were bloodstains on the brickwork outside, but no sign of any in the house, and there were no coal tongs in Edith's room. The doctors were already looking for evidence of foul play and had informed the police. One problem was that the fall in the yard meant that they could not be certain of how Hannah came by at least one of the head injuries.

By the end of Sunday Hannah had slipped into a coma. She gradually faded through the week and died on 21 March. Edith had tried to look after her whilst she was ill, but the post-mortem revealed Hannah had suffered from serious bleeding underneath one of the head wounds and this had compressed her brain. Meningitis had then set in rapidly, and had been the final cause of death.

The gossip had flown around not just Leamington, but even reached the ears of the reporter for the *Birmingham Daily Times*. Mr E Bailley ran a lead article the very next day stating that it was a very suspicious death and the coroner would have to look very carefully into the part that Edith Burbidge had played.

The coroner, Mr D R Wynter had set the inquest for the same day, and he was utterly furious at the way the article appeared to pre-empt his decision. By the time the inquest was due to start at the *Angel Hotel* thousands of people thronged the streets all around. Edith Burbidge arrived in a cart and was loudly hissed by the crowd as she entered.

Mr Wynter opened by criticising the newspaper article, whereupon Mr Bailley stood up and told him that he had every right as a journalist to speculate and report on the case. He wasn't going to have his journalistic freedom curtailed by anyone. Mr Wynter hadn't expected such a robust defence from the newspaper man, and decided to let the matter rest there. More important issues were at stake.

The doctors were the first to give evidence. Both Drs Horniblow and Wilmott stated that one of the head injuries had caused the bleeding and thus Hannah's death. However, neither of them would positively swear that the injury had been caused by a pair of coal tongs, or by falling over in the yard. The massive bruising on Hannah's hands and wrists could have been caused by her trying to fend off the attack by Edith armed with the tongs, but she could have done the damage falling over in the house. P C Rainbow had retrieved a pair of tongs from the house, but the closest examination had revealed no traces of blood on them.

Sarah Graves gave a very confused account of what had happened on the Saturday and Sunday, complete with enough extra gossip to thoroughly blacken Edith's name.

Edith was the last of the witnesses brought before the jury. She told them that Hannah had come into her bedroom at eight on the Saturday morning. She had then tried to take her bottle of brandy away and Edith had stopped her. She did not elaborate on quite how she stopped her. Edith then swore that she didn't see her again for the whole day.

The jury had an awkward decision to make. Edith and Hannah had lived together for twenty years and their constant bickering was legendary. It was quite conceivable that Hannah had fallen over and used the incident to have a go at Edith in just another part of their incessant bickering. It was also possible that Edith really had had enough of the old woman and gone for her with a pair of coal tongs, furiously battering her frail hands out of the way as she went for her head. However, there was no blood on the tongs and plenty of it on the bricks in the yard where Sarah Graves had admitted seeing her fall. Edith may well have had a track record of getting violent when drunk, but that was no proof that on this occasion she had become a murderess.

After a long discussion the jury found that Hannah Smith had died in dubious circumstances, but that there was no evidence to implicate Edith. Mr Wynter duly summed up the case, warned Edith about the perils of drinking to excess, and discharged her. So the question remains: did she or didn't she?

CHAPTER 19

Esther Pardoe: Child Stealer

BIRMINGHAM

1891

I am going to take my sister's child.

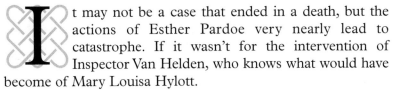

t may not be a case that ended in a death, but the actions of Esther Pardoe very nearly lead to catastrophe. If it wasn't for the intervention of Inspector Van Helden, who knows what would have become of Mary Louisa Hylott.

Esther Pardoe had a boyfriend by the name of Chappell. He wasn't exactly a run of the mill character but an acrobat and itinerant escapologist. He wandered from town to town following the fairs and circuses, performing astounding feats, challenging punters to tie him up and astounding everyone when he wriggled out of the most devious knots they could devise. The trick was to then persuade the astonished audience to chuck their pennies into the hat brought round by an attractive and apparently deserving young girl. Both Chappell and Esther were in their twenties and had no children of their own. It was a problem. As Esther gradually aged the takings in the hat dropped, and they needed to find a child who would tug at the heart strings of their audience.

Esther decided the problem could easily be solved. Her sister had moved away from Birmingham and married Mr Hylott in Tottenham, London, and she had a little girl. In December 1884 Esther visited her sister and, bold as brass, asked for the child. Not surprisingly, Mrs Hylott told her sister very emphatically to forget the idea. Her little four year old was not going away with her. Esther was not so easily dissuaded. She knew another local woman, a friend of both sisters, who lived near by. She visited Mrs Pipkin on 17 December and asked her where the little girl went to school. She didn't attempt to hide what she planned from Mrs Pipkin; she remembered her saying: 'I am going to

A sweet little girl was just what the circus act needed. Strand Magazine

have my sister's child. I asked her to let me have her and she wouldn't; and I want to go to the school to fetch her.'

Mrs Pipkin must have been a bit dim because she then told

Esther that the child was at the Coleraine Park Board School. Some hours later Mrs Hylott turned up at her house in floods of tears saying the child had vanished. The police were called and managed to track Esther down to a local boarding house, but by the time they got there, Esther and the child had gone. The trail went cold.

The years passed with Mary helping Chappell collect his money at the various fairs across the Midlands, living an itinerant life each summer and living with Esther in Birmingham during the winter. She was never sent to school and received no education at home either. She never really knew what her proper name was when she was abducted, and Esther never told her. As far as Mary knew, Esther was her real mother, even though she could vividly remember the day she was taken away from the school. Esther and Chappell did see that she was fed and clothed reasonably well, which was some small mercy.

It all gradually went sour. In the summer of 1890 Chappell was away on tour without Mary, leaving her to the tender care of Esther. The trouble was that she had decided to go off with some of her friends and there wasn't room for Mary. She was turned out onto the street, destitute, penniless and homeless. Mary wandered the streets for days and in desperation went to a Mrs Ball and begged for sustenance. Mrs Ball took pity on the poor eleven-year-old girl and took her in. It was either that or watch her starve to death in the street.

Mrs Ball was by no means a wealthy lady bountiful. She had little enough to share with a starving waif and after about a year she decided she couldn't afford to keep feeding her. She went to the city police and spoke to Chief Inspector Van Helden of the Detective Department. Van Helden started his enquiries and soon discovered that Esther Pardoe had returned to Birmingham and was staying in lodgings in Chapel Street. He took the young girl with him and interviewed Esther.

'I want to know what her name is. She says she does not know what her name is.'

Mary must have been bemused by the revelation that her true name was Mary Louisa Hylott and that Esther was not her real mother. Esther admitted taking her away from the school in London but tried to wriggle out of trouble by asking Mary: 'Have I not always been good to you all the time you have been

Inspector Van Helden was eventually tracked down by the girl's mother.

Strand Magazine

with me?' Mary replied: 'Yes, you have.' It wasn't enough to placate the inspector and Esther was charged with feloniously and fraudulently taking the child with intent to defraud the parents of the possession of the child. Within a couple of days the remarkable affair was being mentioned in newspapers across the country.

In London the story only merited a couple of lines, but by extraordinary good fortune Mrs Hylott managed to spot them. She raced round to the Tottenham police station and begged them to help. They contacted the Birmingham police and mother and child were re-united. By now the Chief Inspector had decided that Mary needed a stable home and education. He had offered her a position as domestic servant in his own household and was arranging for her to get some basic education. Mrs Hylott decided that this was probably better than the life she would have back in Tottenham and seemed content that Mary should live in the luxurious house of Mr Van Helden.

It must have been a close run thing for the little girl, turned out penniless onto the streets of Birmingham. In 1891 it was a dangerous place and she was lucky to survive. Esther Pardoe was committed for trial at the county court and it seems that she received several months' hard labour for her cruel offence.

CHAPTER 20

Abortions

RUGBY AND BIRMINGHAM

1875 and 1893

. . . a sad and melancholy trade . . .

Abortion is never an easy subject, and a book of this nature is not the place for a debate about whether it is right or wrong. There are plenty of other books covering the moral aspect of the matter. That said, it isn't always only the child that is the victim, in Victorian times abortion was illegal and the practice was pushed into the back streets. Indeed one of the arguments for legalisation of the practice is exactly this, exploitative characters preying on desperate pregnant women, putting their lives at risk for a few shillings profit.

In an era before sophisticated drugs, and no antibiotics at all, the operation had an incredibly poor success rate. Nevertheless, one more mouth to feed in an already destitute family led some women to take the risk. Out in the country there was access to a variety of herbs that could be used to induce a miscarriage, although with varying degrees of success. For the women of the city the herbal option was absent and a surgical method of terminating a pregnancy was the only realistic possibility. This latter method grew in numbers as the population shifted from the countryside to the new urban slums. There had been no legislation against abortion in England until this shift between old fashioned herb-induced abortions and the new surgical intervention. In 1803, the first of a series of increasingly harsh laws was passed banning the practice. As the nineteenth century developed, so did the number of back street abortionists.

No one knows just how widespread abortion was. I have seen statistics stating that possibly one birth in five was terminated in the 1890s, which does seem an excessive number, but it is certain that there were many abortionists, and as a result there were also many terminally injured women. By the end of the century it was possible to buy specially designed abortion 'instruments', which may have been a slight improvement on a knitting needle or boot hook, but they were still extremely dangerous to use, even in the hands of an experienced practitioner. Much more detail than this is probably best left out.

It seems fairly certain that as long as nothing went wrong the police left the whole sorry business well alone. There weren't that many police and they had their hands full with all the other villains that appear in these books. What does appear from the records of the era is that when things did go wrong the police would prosecute and the judiciary would hand out some very severe sentences. However, there are very few records of anyone being prosecuted solely for being an abortionist in nineteenth century Warwickshire.

Two cases in 1875 show how mid-Victorian society reacted to abortion. In the market town of Rugby, Mary Ann Billingham (not a relation of mine I hasten to add) was arrested in April. The local surgeon had attended one of her clients, Eliza Renshaw. Eliza was a twenty-year-old barmaid at the *Avon Inn* and had found she was pregnant in February. She made several visits to Mrs Billingham's house in James Street and during one of these visits Mrs Billingham had used a specialist abortion instrument on her. Quite how much Eliza paid for this treatment was not recorded, but her subsequent illness certainly was. The local surgeon, Mr Duke Ingram, attended her and delivered a very premature baby, about three months gestation. Eliza was now dreadfully ill and hovered on the brink of death for a week or so. Mr Ingram was not in the least impressed. What made matters worse was that Eliza was by no means the only girl in the same situation. Sarah Crofts and Ruth Bromwich had also had abortions that had gone horribly wrong. All three girls were encouraged to press charges against Mary Billingham. They were likely to face prosecution themselves if they didn't.

Mary Billingham was no gin swigging old crone eking out some precarious life.

The sinister side of Victorian society, the secret world of abortion. Strand Magazine

She was quite wealthy, married to Thomas and fifty-two years old. She even had her own servant, Emily Webb. She had been carrying on her trade for many years and society in Rugby had taken no action against her. Now though, even her servant was interrogated. Emily finally admitted that once all three girls became ill, Mary gave her the 'instrument' with instructions to hide it away until the trouble died down.

If Emily had not handed over the instrument to the police, she would have been looking after it for a long time. The judge at the Summer Session of the Warwickshire Assizes described her crime as '... a sad and melancholy trade which furnished unhappy people with the means of getting rid of unwanted offspring'. He then sentenced Mary Ann Billingham to twenty years in prison.

Mary Billingham's case doesn't give us much idea of the prevalence of abortion. Emily Webb told the court that several

Twenty years of Warwick Gaol was as effective as any death sentence. Most prisoners would be dead of Gaol fever inside ten. The author

persons came to Mrs Billingham for 'medical treatment' every week. This could amount to about a hundred abortions per annum for a population of 9,000, or very roughly one abortion per ten live births. That figure is assuming that Mary Billingham was the only abortionist in town.

If the sentence of twenty years handed down to Mary Billingham was supposed to deter anyone from carrying on with illegal abortions, it was utterly unsuccessful. Later that year an old lady in Birmingham was prosecuted for performing abortions and her case gives us slightly more information surrounding this dubious trade.

Jane Wilkinson was sixty years old when it all went wrong. She was a widow; her husband had been a druggist. She had worked as a 'female' doctor specialising in various women's ailments, you can guess which ones. When her husband died she carried on with her trade alone, keeping the house and shop in Summer Lane. It was to the side door of this establishment that Charlotte Tidman and her sister made their furtive way on 26 July. Jane Wilkinson had made them swear an oath of secrecy as to the nature of the treatment. Charlotte Tidman was in a difficult position, her husband was away in America, and had been for rather longer than the age of her unborn child.

There was a certain amount of quibbling about the cost. Jane wanted £5, which was way beyond the means of Charlotte. Jane told her that a lady would have to pay at least £20, but eventually settled for £2 10s. It was several weeks wages for Charlotte, but she had few options open now. If her husband returned to find her pregnant he could quite legally throw her out onto the streets for adultery.

She was healthy enough and at twenty-eight, strong enough to withstand the barbaric surgery that she had to endure. Jane Wilkinson laid her out on the counter and used that ferocious 'instrument' on her, killing the child inside her womb. Charlotte never saw the instrument, but heard it clang when Jane dropped it on the floor. Hardly hygienic, and not only did Charlotte miscarry soon afterwards, but she also developed a life threatening infection within a few days.

After several weeks Charlotte was so seriously ill that she feared for her life. Mr Lawson Tait, the local surgeon, examined her confirmed that she had suffered a miscarriage, although he would not say whether or not it had been artificially induced. As she weakened and became convinced she was going to die, Charlotte called for the local policeman, PC Cooper, and told him what had happened. She did rather edit the story, so perhaps this wasn't the real deathbed confession that it was later purported to be. She told him that she had only visited Jane Wilkinson for an examination, and she had performed the abortion without her consent. Nobody really believed a word of that bit of her story, although there wasn't any questioning of the rest of it.

Charlotte eventually recovered. She had been confined to bed for sixteen weeks and at several stages came very close to death. The prosecution of Jane Wilkinson for procuring an abortion came to court on 18 December. Charlotte's deathbed confession was enough to convict Jane. PC Cooper was further questioned and stated that he knew that Jane had been carrying out these 'illegal operations' for many years and had once searched the premises after a tip-off. He had not found the dreaded 'instrument' and had thus let the matter rest.

For Jane Wilkinson, who had carried on this trade virtually unmolested for years, the sentence was catastrophic. The jury had recommended mercy on account of her age, and the judge duly gave her just seven years in prison. It was the equivalent of a death sentence for this old lady. She was dragged from the court screaming: 'I am an innocent woman! I am a murdered woman! I shall never come out again.'

Matters didn't improve as the century wore on. There was still no effective contraception but passions ran as deep as ever. It was in the poverty struck slums that the back street abortionists found most of their custom; not over enthusiastic single girls but ordinary married women who just couldn't afford another mouth to feed. Not only was there no contraception, but they had no way to prevent their husbands exercising their marital rights (short of a spot of arsenic or some of the techniques described in this book). Basically, women had fewer rights in the nineteenth century than their husband's pet dog.

On 19 April 1893 Elizabeth Cooper waited until her husband, Frederick, left for work and then put into action the plan she had been secretly harbouring. The two of them lived in a shoddy court, one of twelve tenement style back to backs at the rear of Berners Street. These places were squalid beyond imagining, all twelve families sharing a water pump in the yard, with virtually no privacy amid paper thin walls. Elizabeth had decided that it was no place to bring a baby up and would risk an abortion. With her husband safely out at work she called over one of the lads, Ernest Pearson, and told him to go and find Elizabeth Corbett, and get her to bring 'the woman' to her. Corbett was a machinist in a local factory and 'the woman' was Elizabeth Perry, generally described as a charwoman, but one with special skills.

Elizabeth Cooper was in good health and only twenty-four years of age. She doesn't appear to have had any worries about the health of the foetus other than the dreadful conditions in which the family was forced to survive. At the time the mortality rate for children born into the slums of the city was staggeringly high, even the adults were lucky if they reached forty-five. Corbett and Perry duly arrived at the house and Perry used a specially designed hook needle to destroy the foetus, all without anaesthetic or hygienic conditions. You really don't want to know any more detail than that. The wicked pair then took the money and left.

Frederick Cooper returned from work to find his wife dreadfully ill and screaming in agony. Early the next morning he sent for the local midwife, Rachael Gaelford. Rachael examined Elizabeth and realised she had just had a miscarriage. It struck her as a bit odd and she asked the girl what had happened. Elizabeth told her that she had strained herself while washing. Rachael was not entirely convinced, but there was little in the way of treatment she could give her.

Elizabeth grew steadily more ill, an infection was burning through her whole system. By the 25 April Rachael was called back, but there was little hope, Elizabeth was running a high fever and completely delirious. Some of her neighbours, Mrs Pearson and Mrs Heale, sat with her trying to ease her suffering. Through the long night and into the cold dawn Elizabeth made little sense, but the fever seemed to abate during the 26th and she told the two women exactly what had happened, and that it was Elizabeth Perry who had killed her. Elizabeth Cooper felt she was definitely dying and wanted to charge Perry with her murder whilst she still could. She rallied briefly through that afternoon, but the next night saw her descend once more into delirium and fever. The next day she died.

Mrs Heale and Mrs Parsons went straight to the police and made sworn statements about what Elizabeth had told them. Both Corbett and Perry were arrested as a result. Some weeks later they were hauled up before the Warwick Quarter Sessions accused of wilful murder and a second charge of the illegal use of instruments.

As the case proceeded it was looking pretty bleak for them. Corbett had managed to get a lawyer to defend her, but Perry had to rely on the duty lawyer, Mr Raymond. When the evidence reached the point where the dying statement of Elizabeth Cooper was due to be read out, the defence counsel objected, saying that it was not made in the present fear of death since she had rallied a little after making it. A second objection was that there was some question as to whether she was in full possession of her mental faculties at the time.

The judge retired to contemplate the exact position of the law in relation to this objection. After ten minutes he returned and gave his judgement. The dying statement of Elizabeth Cooper was not made in the present fear of death, without even the hope of continuance of life. The statement could not be used as evidence. To the horror of almost everyone in the court the entire charge of murder collapsed. The prosecution then decided to abandon the second charge and the two women walked from the court room, free, but reviled by all who saw them.

All in all, the banning of abortion doesn't seem to have reduced its incidence during the nineteenth century, and it certainly led to an uncontrolled cadre of incompetent practitioners who left a trail of wounded and dead women, as well as foetuses. Quite what lessons this has for the twenty-first century I will leave to the politicians and churchmen.

A PROSECUTION FOR MURDER BREAKS DOWN. — Elizabeth Perry (42), charwoman, and Elizabeth Corbett (36), machinist, were indicted for the wilful murder of Elizabeth Cooper, at Aston, on April 27th.— Mr. J. S. Dugdale, Q.C., and Mr. Stanger prosecuted; Mr. Hugo Young defended Corbett; and Mr. Raymond at the request of the judge defended Perry.— Mr. Dugdale said the case would depend upon whether the jury were satisfied that prisoners attempted to procure an illegal result on the person of the deceased, Elizabeth Cooper. Evidence would be given to the death of Elizabeth Cooper having been caused by an illegal operation,

CHAPTER 21

Bridget Gavin
STOURBRIDGE
1895

The workhouse system provided an answer
to their problems.

One of the darker facets of Victorian life was the workhouse. Social Security was virtually non-existent and if you lost your job or became ill there was no provision for you. It was a matter of starving to death or going to the workhouse. These dark forbidding institutions grew up in the early decades of the century and provided a minimum of food and shelter for their unfortunate inmates. The sexes were housed separately and the children kept apart from their parents. Mindlessly dull work filled every day, picking oakum and similar tedious and often painful tasks were designed as much to keep the inmates busy as to produce a worthwhile product. The children were given an education, but in conditions that would make even the most heartless quail. The workhouse masters and matrons frequently had a reputation for sadistic bullying, sexual exploitation and general neglect of the vulnerable souls entrusted to their dubious care. In such an era of ruthless manipulation of the poor, it took only a minor illness to render a family destitute.

For the Gavin family, recently arrived from Ireland, it was a major tragedy that sent them into a spiral of decline. Mrs Gavin died leaving her husband with two young daughters to support on wages that were barely sufficient to feed himself. John Gavin took the unavoidable but drastic step of sending the two girls, Bridget and Margaret, to the workhouse at Stourbridge. It meant that they would not starve to death, but it also meant that they became the virtual property of the workhouse.

Not far from Knowle, near Solihull, was a farm called Waterfield. Here the Greaves family managed a few dozen acres

Waterfield Farm lies just across the fields from the canal. The author

and raised their family in very different circumstances. Mr and Mrs Greaves were a well liked couple, regular church goers, and considered generous and kind hearted by the local community. Agriculture in this period was in serious decline with cheap imported food pushing farm prices down. It was all they could manage to pay the few labourers that they had, but they still needed someone to help with the housework and looking after their young children. The workhouse system provided an answer to their problems. They could house, clothe and feed a girl who would otherwise be a burden on the workhouse. So it was that in 1893 Mrs Greaves came home from a trip to Stourbridge with Bridget Gavin, their new domestic servant.

Bridget Gavin was fifteen, quite stout and probably emotionally scarred from her experiences in the workhouse. She was not the brightest button in the box either. Bridget settled down to life in the Greaves household, doing the washing and cleaning, looking after the youngest children, Violet and Percy, and at first all went smoothly. Bridget took to baby Violet well and was really fond of her.

A year passed and Mr and Mrs Greaves were starting to have faint suspicions about Bridget. Small amounts of money were going missing from their children's purses and postage stamps were vanishing from the office desk. Bridget was also turning out to be pretty hopeless at the housework. She bustled about looking busy, but somehow things just didn't get done. Mrs Greaves found a letter from Bridget's sister, Margaret, still in Stourbridge Workhouse. In the letter she thanked Bridget for the money she had sent. Alarm bells rang and Mrs Greaves tackled Bridget about it. Bridget denied everything even though four shillings had disappeared a few weeks before. Bridget may have been fed and clothed, but she was paid no money at all for her services. She should not have had any money to send to Margaret. Mrs Greaves first wrote to Margaret for confirmation and then took the matter up with the matron of the workhouse. The matron told Mrs Greaves that Bridget would simply be thrown out onto the street if she lost her position at the farm. Mrs Greaves was a bit too soft hearted to take such a drastic step and so Bridget stayed at the farm.

By March 1895 things had become a lot worse. Small amounts of cash had continued to vanish and on the 20th the oldest son lost his purse. Mr Greaves gave Bridget a stern talking to and accused her of stealing it. He even threatened to call in the local policeman, Constable Court. She denied this theft hotly and after a search of the house the purse turned up under the boy's mattress. The money was still inside it.

Bridget knew she was on borrowed time with the Greaves. A few weeks before she had written a letter to her father, enclosing postage stamps to the value of ten shillings, in it she mentioned her sister and said: 'I sometimes send her money.' The letter went on: 'I shall be soon leaving my place I am sorry to say because my mistress is so fond of me and I have not had one cross word off her since I have been here. Can I come and stay with you until I get another place?' It seems there was no reply to this plea.

The following morning Mrs Greaves decided that enough was enough and before she went off to Birmingham for the day, told Bridget that she would have to find another place very

THE KNOWLE MYSTERY.

SUPPOSED MURDER AND SUICIDE.

It was reported in yesterday's *Post* that a Birmingham boatman had discovered in the canal, near Knowle, the body of Violet Iris Greaves, the two year daughter of Mr. Joseph Greaves, of Waterfield Farm. The child had been taken out for a walk on the previous day by a servant named Bridget Gavin, who had not returned, and whose disappearance gave a sinister interpretation to a remark that she made to another child of Mr. Greaves just before she took the baby out: "Good bye; we shan't come back again." When the child's body was found it was surmised that Gavin had either thrown it into the water and decamped, or that she had committed suicide by leaping into the water with it in her arms. The canal was therefore dragged by the police during Thursday evening without result, but search was resumed yesterday morning by Police-constables Constable and Court, under the direction of Inspector Carbis, and after three hours' dragging Gavin's body was brought to the surface not very far

Warwickshire Advertiser

soon. Bridget was left on her own from ten. She made a few desultory efforts at the housework and fed the children their dinner around lunchtime. Quite what was going through her mind we will never understand. She was clearly in danger of losing her job and home, and possibly even risked prosecution for theft if she was caught again. Whether she was angry or depressed no one will ever know.

After feeding Violet and Percy their lunch, Bridget told four-year-old Percy that Violet and her were going out with the pet pig Ginnie. Percy probably wanted to go as well, but Bridget promised him a pistol if he stayed at home. Percy didn't realise the dreadful import of her parting words to him: 'Me and Violet are going to drown ourselves and we are taking Ginnie along.'

The four-year-old lad duly stayed at home, completely unaware of the dreadful meaning of those words, perhaps he just thought it was a new game. Outside, Samuel Cattrell, a local carpenter, saw Bridget leading the little toddler across the field towards the Warwick and Birmingham Canal. This was nothing

A modern holiday boat cruises past the scene of the tragedy. The author

unusual, Bridget often took the four-year-old up to the bridge to watch the brightly painted boats slide gracefully by. Samuel spoke to Bridget but she just turned her head away, looking confused. As they carried on across the field, followed by the scampering pet pig, Samuel shrugged and got on with his work.

An hour later Sidney Harris was at the helm of his narrow boat, the horse slowly plodding along the towpath, when he saw something floating in the water not far from the bridge by Waterfield Farm. It was the body of a toddler. He tied up the boat and ran across to the farm to raise the alarm. Within a few minutes the sad little body had been pulled out of the water and identified as that of Violet Iris Greaves. The police were called and at first Constable Court suspected that Bridget must have thrown the child into the canal as revenge and then run away. His fellow officer was not so sure, knowing that Bridget was very fond of the child. They searched along the canal to see if there was anything more to be found.

In the failing light they spotted Bridget's hat floating in the water about two hundred yards away. It was beginning to look as though Bridget may well have drowned herself as well. At first light the next morning they started to drag the canal. Inspector Carbis and Violet's father, Joseph Greaves, watched intently as, yard-by-yard, the muddy depths of the canal were dragged. After three hours the two constables finally located and dragged the body of Bridget Gavin to the bank not far from where Violet had been found. Bridget was found with her arms folded across her chest as though she was still holding the child.

The coroner's inquest was held the next day. The verdict was that Bridget had wilfully murdered Violet and then committed suicide whilst temporarily insane. It was accurate as far as it went, but who knows whether Bridget was mad or bad? Was she so terrified of returning to the workhouse that she decided death in the cold waters of the canal was easier, and took the only person who loved her unreservedly along with her on that unknown dark journey?

The inquest was held at the Greswolde Hotel *in nearby Knowle.* The author

Chapter 22

Jennie Wilstrop
Balsall Heath
1896

I have done it and I don't care.

Alfred Brooks ran off to join the army in 1886. He left not only his family in Balsall Heath, but also his teenage sweetheart, Jennie Wilstrop. He was only eighteen and soon found that he wasn't cut out to be a soldier. He lacked the fighting spirit and barely controlled aggression that was so necessary for an army defending a worldwide empire. He was a lad with a mild temperament, an easy going nature and a tendency to avoid conflict rather than face it and fight. It was easy enough to join the army, the recruiting sergeants were anything but choosy; but once signed up to a regiment there was only one way to get out, he would have to buy his way back to civvy street. This was an expensive option but Jennie came to his aid and paid the regiment £20 for his release. It was a huge sum of money then, but she managed to scrape it together somehow.

Once Alfred was out of the army the two of them moved into a house together and by 1888 were a settled couple. Alfred got himself a job as a bus driver with Messers Norst & Young. It was a good steady job, and for a while everything was looking fine. The Birmingham buses of the day were small, usually with an open upper deck, and pulled by a pair of strong cart horses. As the city grew rapidly so did the demand for economic public transport and yet another industry thrived.

Jennie had something of a temper and a particularly unforgiving streak. Gradually their passion faded and they split up in 1891. Alfred moved to lodgings in Orchard Street and hoped to start over again. Jennie was absolutely livid about it all, if nothing else he hadn't ever paid her back the £20 she raised to buy him out of the army. She wasn't going to let the relationship just fade away, her passion turned to a violent hatred just as intense.

Alfred had a very predictable job, his route every day was along Hurst Street in the centre of Birmingham and through the suburbs out to Hall Green. The bus crews were all fairly close friends. For most of the time John Vears was the conductor on Alfred's bus and John Thulbourne was the groom who looked after the horses. It wasn't long before everyone knew that Alfred had got a real problem with Jennie.

Almost every evening Jennie would be walking around Hurst Street, and if the bus passed by she would start shouting and swearing at Alfred, and anyone on board. If she had had a few drinks the whole street soon knew about it all. Most evenings she went for a few drinks in a variety of beer houses and soon met some very dubious characters. After a year Jennie's passionate hatred had hardened into a vicious core of sheer malice. One evening she saw Alfred and John Thulbourne chatting away to some girls on the bus. The very thought of Alfred having the chance of another relationship was absolutely galling. She went into one of her regular haunts and managed to persuade a local gang to catch Alfred and beat him up. The attack happened just after Alfred and John finished for the night. Jennie and the gang were waiting for them outside the depot. John and Alfred ran for their lives as the gang hammered down the road after them, sparks flying from their steelshod boots on the cobbles. They were shouting that they would kill both the drivers.

Alfred and John managed to slip into Caldicott's stables and hide in the chaff room. The gang roamed the streets all night, leaving them to spend the whole night hiding amongst the bales and sacks of chaff. They had to creep stealthily home in the grey light of dawn. Fortunately the matter seems to have blown over and the gang didn't try any further attacks. The same couldn't be said for Jennie.

By the spring of 1893 Jennie was behaving more and more violently. One night she jumped onto the bus and started hitting and kicking a girl that she wrongly thought had been talking to Alfred. Almost every night she would walk up and down the street yelling insults at his bus whenever it came past. On 16 May she completely lost her temper when she found Alfred and a group of other drivers coming out of Day's Concert Hall in Hurst Street. She ran across the road shrieking at him: 'This is your bloody game. I see you've got your tykes with you tonight.' She slashed at him with her umbrella, hitting him twice. She then ran off a few paces. Alfred told the others to ignore her, but she followed them to Macdonald Street. Luckily for Alfred there were two policemen there and they promptly arrested her. She was charged, fined £5 and bound over to keep the peace.

The shock of her arrest calmed Jennie down for a while but by August 1895 she was back to her old vitriolic tricks. She had another go at Alfred with her brolly, but this time his patience finally snapped and he belted her back. The police were once again involved and the magistrates heard the case on the 7th. Alfred was fined just 2 shillings and sixpence, with 10 shillings costs. Jennie probably felt even more hard done by after this and her tirades against him continued most evenings.

The 18 May 1896 was Race Day at Hall Green. This was long before the dog track was built, and the racecourse was simply a very large field and home to all sorts of racing. Thousands of people flocked out of the grimy black city streets to the relative rural peace of Hall Green for a grand day out. Beer tents and stalls were set up along the road, bookies and fortune tellers rubbed shoulders with everyone from boatmen to bankers. Every spare bus in the city shuttled the teeming throngs back and forth from the city centre. Alfred and his fellow driver James Brueton arrived at the racecourse and parked up

Horse-drawn buses were the principal public transport within the city.
Author's collection

their omnibuses. They were going to be there for a couple of hours so they arranged with the conductors that they would take turns to look after the horses. The two drivers set off into the bustling mass of people.

After twenty minutes Alfred muttered something to James and promptly sprinted off up the field. Jennie Wilstrop was running after him, taking pebbles from her pocket and flinging them at him as she ran. William Smith, the fruiterer from Kerwick's Lane heard her shout in his direction: 'I bought him out of the army and he's been calling me a cow.'

She yelled at Alfred as she pursued him across the grass: 'I'm on your track this time my lad.'

Alfred ran out of the field and stopped. Jennie surged through the crowd and hit him hard across the face with the back of her hand. Alfred slapped her back, knocking the hat off her head on the second blow. William Smith decided that the blows were not particularly hard and didn't intervene. The press of the crowd was now so strong that Alfred and Jennie were forced apart. It was only a temporary lull in Jennie's one woman war.

Alfred bumped into James and the two of them decided it was high time they went back to the buses and let the guards have their turn at wandering around the race course. Alfred's fun day at the races was turning pretty sour. Across the crowd Jennie bumped back into William Smith, who told her that it was race day and to enjoy herself.

She retorted: 'I mean to do for him today and if I can't do it on the course I'll drop a brick on the bus.'

William Howlett was near Jennie and William Smith as the crush of people gradually edged them towards the tents on the side of the course. 'I'll get my own back,' she muttered, just as a gap appeared in the crowd. Her words slid through the suddenly open space - and there was her nemesis, Alfred, walking just yards away from her.

'You have knocked me about, haven't you, and I'll get my own back tonight.'

He turned his head back and sneered at her, saying: 'Good luck to you.'

In a wild fury Jennie leapt across the field and, gripping her umbrella with both hands, lunged at Alfred's face. He flung up his arm to ward off the blow, but was too late. Her sturdy arms drove the point of the brolly into his cheek, in and in, right up to the silk.

'Oh, my eye, my eye.' Alfred staggered against James and started to collapse as Jennie wrenched the umbrella from his shattered face. She turned to the stunned witnesses and dropped the brolly. She said to William Howlett: 'Now you can have me pinched, you can send for who you like now. I have done it and I don't care.'

Alfred slowly slid to the ground, blood flowing from the small, but incredibly deep wound in his cheek. He gradually lost consciousness. James and the other bus drivers carried him onto a bus and took him home, alerting his mother and a doctor on the way. Jennie disappeared into the crowd.

No one realised quite how seriously injured Alfred was. When James Brueton left him he was starting to vomit blood. The point of the umbrella had punched straight through his upper jaw bone underneath his eye; it had penetrated the base of his skull and cut into his brain. Dr Joseph Patrick came round that evening and found he was in a state of shock and had lost a lot of blood, but he couldn't do much for the small external wound. Alfred's mother, Susan Brooks, arrived the next morning and found him very poorly indeed; she decided to stay and nurse him.

Alfred seemed to make a bit of a recovery through the next week but he was still very ill. Jennie had carried on life as though nothing had happened, but on 29 of May Inspector William Parkinson of Acocks Green called at her house, 101 Hope Street, and charged her with assaulting Alfred Brooks.

'I am guilty, I have been expecting you.'

The inspector took her to the station, and then returned on 1 June to collect her umbrellas as evidence.

On 3 June Alfred started to run a fever and rapidly weakened. Tiny particles of dirt and bacteria had been on the tip of the umbrella, and, in a world without antibiotics, had gradually become a lethal infection. For fifteen hours Alfred writhed in agony, his brain inflamed and his system poisoned. He died on the morning of 4 June.

Who would have thought that a brolley could be so lethal? Strand Magazine

Dr Patrick performed a post-mortem the next day. Jennie was in the city prison on the charge of assault. The doctor needed to determine whether she was also responsible for Alfred's death. The post-mortem revealed the true extent of the damage her umbrella had done. Inspector Parkinson went to the prison the next day and charged Jennie with causing Alfred's death. She told him she had hit at him with her brown umbrella, but it was in self defence.

Jennie Wilstrop pleaded not guilty to the charge of murder when she was brought before the magistrates on 19 June. They referred the case to the main Quarter Sessions held at Warwick. It was here that she was found guilty of manslaughter. There wasn't sufficient evidence that the attack was a premeditated attempt to deliberately kill Alfred, but plenty of evidence that she caused his death. She was sentenced to eight months hard labour.

Epilogue

So, after six months research, are there any dramatic conclusions about female killers in the nineteenth century? Well, they are just as daft, nasty or malicious as the men. 'Daft' crops up quite often. Elizabeth Blower was the twenty-year-old servant of Mr Felthouse in Tamworth. She decided to give the baby a dose of laudanum to keep it quiet. In this it worked all too successfully and she had to run away once the baby died later that night. She only ran as far as her father's house and was arrested for poisoning the child the following day. The jury decided that she was not guilty of intending to kill the child, and discharged her. Quite what Mr and Mrs Felthouse made of the matter was unrecorded, but it is fairly certain that she was dismissed.

'Nasty' occurs repeatedly. Very, very nasty in some cases. The institution of the workhouse was prevalent all through the nineteenth century and it had the effect of brutalising the poor. It was an ever present reminder of the power of the state, from birth to death. Some characters rebelled in curious ways. Ann Lole of Foleshill, Coventry, was confined for her childbirth in the local workhouse in 1862. The baby was born fit and well, and she was sent home with some dole money to help her for the first month. Ann thought this was grossly unfair, in a world without contraception, and with abortion completely illegal, she felt oppressed and exploited by the system. The charity money stopped after a month and her comment was 'The b——s shall not have the laugh on me, I would choose the gallows first.' She came very close to the second option when she brought the child back to the workhouse. Joe Orton, the medical officer there, found the baby had horrific scalds all over its legs. Ann told him it must be an illness called 'Blister Pock'. Mr Orton had spent most of his life working with miners and steam engine drivers and was absolutely convinced that this was no illness but burns and scalds. He refused to treat the child until she admitted what had happened. This she refused. In a few days the child had died and the post-mortem revealed what appeared to be massive scalds across virtually all the baby's skin, far more than when Mr Orton had first examined it. Such was the primitive state of medical knowledge in 1862 that the jury were unable to determine whether these were real scalds or some illness. Ann Lole managed to faint fairly dramatically during the hearing, and eventually walked free from the court.

Malicious, well, you've read plenty of those by now.

Overall, women in the nineteenth century were incredibly restrained considering the way that they were treated by society, beaten by their husbands and classified as little more than beasts of burden by the law. The real surprise is that there have been so few cases to research...

To sleep perchance to die. . . Strand Magazine

And so farewell. Strand Magazine

Principal Sources

Warwickshire Advertiser & Leamington Gazette held at Shakespeare Birthplace Trust Records Office and Warwickshire County Library.

Old & New Birmingham, R K Dent

Strand Magazine

TRUE CRIME FROM WHARNCLIFFE

Foul Deeds and Suspicious Deaths Series

Barking, Dagenham & Chadwell Heath
Barnsley
Bath
Bedford
Birmingham
Black Country
Blackburn and Hyndburn
Bolton
Bradford
Brighton
Bristol
Cambridge
Carlisle
Chesterfield
Colchester
Coventry
Croydon
Derby
Dublin
Durham
Ealing
Folkestone and Dover
Grimsby
Guernsey
Guildford
Halifax
Hampstead, Holborn and St Pancras
Huddersfield
Hull

Leeds
Leicester
Lewisham and Deptford
Liverpool
London's East End
London's West End
Manchester
Mansfield
More Foul Deeds Birmingham
More Foul Deeds Chesterfield
More Foul Deeds Wakefield
Newcastle
Newport
Norfolk
Northampton
Nottingham
Oxfordshire
Pontefract and Castleford
Portsmouth
Rotherham
Scunthorpe
Southend-on-Sea
Staffordshire and The Potteries
Stratford and South Warwickshire
Tees
Warwickshire
Wigan
York

OTHER TRUE CRIME BOOKS FROM WHARNCLIFFE

A-Z of Yorkshire Murder
Black Barnsley
Brighton Crime and Vice 1800-2000
Durham Executions
Essex Murders
Executions & Hangings in Newcastle
    and Morpeth
Norfolk Mayhem and Murder

Norwich Murders
Strangeways Hanged
The A-Z of London Murders
Unsolved Murders in Victorian and
    Edwardian London
Unsolved Norfolk Murders
Unsolved Yorkshire Murders
Yorkshire's Murderous Women

Please contact us via any of the methods below for more information or a catalogue.

WHARNCLIFFE BOOKS

47 Church Street – Barnsley – South Yorkshire – S70 2AS
Tel: 01226 734555 – 734222 Fax: 01226 – 734438
E-mail: enquiries@pen-and-sword.co.uk
Website: www.wharncliffebooks.co.uk

Index